# Have You Eaten?

Deliciously Simple Asian Cooking
For Every Mood

# Have You Eaten?

## VERNA GAO

# CONTENTS
CONTENTS

CONTENTS

CONTENTS

CONTENTS

CONTENTS

CONTENTS

# Have You Eaten?

Those three words – have you eaten? – are commonly asked when you first meet someone. I most certainly always ask this...

Having moved to the UK at the age of nine, my prominent childhood memories of food in China were before that age. I remember fondly watching my mum or grandparents gather in a small, cramped kitchen to cook, especially on occasions like Chinese New Year or the Mid-Autumn Festival – food always made us happy. This will come as no surprise to many, since food is at the heart of Chinese culture. I'll even go as far to say it is the centrepiece of many Asian cultures. It's undoubtedly the first thing people think about when any special occasion approaches. It's food that brings everyone together, not drink – probably because many Asians are unfortunately allergic to alcohol, but generally not to food, thankfully.

So, it makes sense that learning about food is important, especially traditional kitchen skills such as pleating dumplings or making a good broth, and formed an influential part of my life. Saying that, it may come as a surprise to find out that I didn't learn a whole lot about cooking from my family growing up. As a child in China, your one and only responsibility is to study and get good grades. Being an only child, as with many other families, none of us were tasked with the duty of looking after ourselves. That was what our parents were there for. Even if they never verbally expressed that they loved us, the sheer act of cooking up fresh and nutritious meals every day was enough. That's how we Asians typically express love. You'll be hard pressed to find an Asian parent who freely says the words, "I love you", but you'll easily experience one asking, "Have you eaten?" as a way of figuring out what they can do to make you feel better.

Those three words  – have you eaten? – are also commonly asked when you first meet someone. I most certainly always ask this as

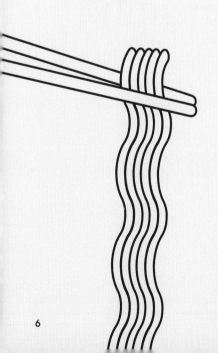

I want to know if my friends are hungry or are in the mood to eat, or whether our time together can involve some kind of food. After all, to me and many others, food always makes life better.

Yet, despite not formally learning how to make all the classic Chinese dishes from my family when young, I enjoyed following the adults around the food markets as they shopped for ingredients. I would also often hover in, or near, the kitchen as the smell of cooking diffused into other rooms of our house before mealtimes. I loved watching different ingredients being thrown into the wok and the cooking sounds emanating from it, lots of sizzling and bubbling, along with the noise that came with chopping and crushing ingredients and stirring of pots. It's kind of magical how simple ingredients picked up at the market could be transformed into delicious dishes that in time have become many of my own home favourites.

One of the most memorable and important skills I did learn from my grandma, however, was how to pleat dumplings. She made them beautifully, and I can still remember her holding my hand to demonstrate the technique.

After moving to London as a child, I went through many years despising my identity, and would reluctantly admit to being Chinese if I was asked. This was mostly due to the negative stereotypes associated with being Chinese, as well as the belief by many that Chinese food was cheap, greasy and unhealthy. There would also be the inevitable mention of sweet-and-sour chicken (a dish that I may have eaten only twice in my life) despite Chinese cuisine having so many more amazing dishes to offer.

My attitude towards my own culture's food changed and developed throughout my teenage years when I realized how much more there was to Chinese cooking. Aside from the typical dishes found in Chinese takeaways, it frustrated me how little variety there was to be found outside of China. Not only that, so much of the food that I grew up eating was misunderstood, or simply unknown.

Having gone to university and unintentionally wowed my flatmates and friends with simple yet delicious meals I was able to make on a budget, I started teaching those around me my easy recipes, like classic egg-fried rice. I recall one evening in my first year when I gathered fourteen of my flatmates in the kitchen to show them how to cook "real Chinese food". This was after watching them order a Chinese takeaway that was less than lacklustre in

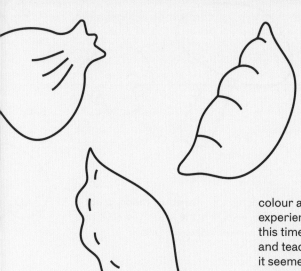

colour and flavour – I felt almost embarrassed that this was their experience of food from my country of birth. I think it was around this time that I realized I was able to spread a bit more knowledge and teach others about the food I enjoyed growing up, even if it seemed simple and obvious to me. It also became clear that most students knew very little about how to eat well, especially on a tight budget.

This continued to ring true after I graduated and started work. When I moved into flatshares as a young twenty-something starting a career in London, I often shared kitchens with others who weren't sure of how to cook – of course, I happily fed them whenever possible, offering them a taste of this or that when I made a meal they seemed interested in. And, if they appeared to be a fan, I would feel a real sense of accomplishment and go into recipe sharing mode, even though I never once measured my ingredients up till that point. This is probably why writing the recipes in this book has been such a different ball game for me, since I meticulously used my measuring spoons and scales while testing everything.

My obsession with food wasn't just in the dishes I cooked at home, it was also a priority whenever and wherever I travelled – from hunting down authentic delicacies to slurping noodles while grazing elbows with locals, and dining at some of the world's most renowned restaurants. I wanted to experience and learn about how people around the world made food irresistible and delicious and how I could implement these skills at home.

So when the pandemic hit and most pondered what they were going to do with all the time on their hands while being at home 24/7, without any lengthy consideration I immediately knew. I was going to cook. Everything that I was no longer able to easily get dining out, I was going to try and cook myself at home.

At first it was just a distraction. While my housemates binged countless series on Netflix and bought gaming devices, I occupied the kitchen and cooked three meals a day. Yes, it was as exhausting, if not more so, than it sounds. I scoured the internet for cooking equipment, pretty bowls and plates, different props and cutlery just so everything from the food to aesthetics would be perfect. It became my creative outlet. Without realizing, the pandemic provided me with an unexpected and brilliant platform for showcasing my recipes and cooking.

Over time, this became a collection of more and more vibrant and delicious recipes that gave people around the world through social media an easy insight into Asian cuisine. Most focused on accessible Chinese cooking, while others involved dishes that I loved and were inspired by places I had travelled to. And as my followers grew, so did my desire to recreate even more exciting dishes to both challenge myself and satisfy my taste buds. Through documenting the process and showing beautifully presented final dishes, I have been able to teach hundreds of thousands of people how easy it is to cook delicious Asian food.

With many people now regularly making my dishes and my audience sharing their tags and take on a recipe, I've become really proud of how it's become a go-to platform for many when it comes to Asian recipe inspiration, especially dishes that are vibrant, simple and healthy.

All the recipes you find in this cookbook reflect this – beautifully presented, flavourful Asian dishes that are easy to make and sumptuous to eat. Aside from that, each dish has been carefully curated to address a reader's needs or how they might be feeling. In a rush with just a few ingredients to hand? Try my Shanghai Spring Onion Oil Noodles (see p.42). Need some comfort food? Then my Beef Ho Fun (see p.128) may be exactly what you're looking for.

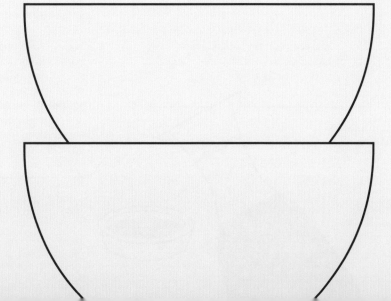

# Ingredients

Before we begin cooking, let's talk about a few of my most used and favourite ingredients that you will find in the recipes in this book.

Most of you are no doubt familiar with popular ingredients, such as soy sauce, in Asian cooking, but there's so much more. I always like to stock up on the following as they're versatile and can easily be found in the world food aisle in mainstream supermarkets or, better still, in your local Asian grocers.

If the idea of venturing into an Asian grocer sounds a little intimidating, allow me to walk you through the ingredients, brands and bottles you should look for. I got you!

## OYSTER SAUCE

A condiment commonly used in Chinese cooking is oyster sauce. It has a richer, thicker consistency than soy sauce and is dark brown in appearance. As its name suggests, good-quality oyster sauce is made from real oyster extract. That said, it has a slightly sweet, salty flavour, rather than a strong taste of shellfish.

For my vegan friends in the room, look for mushroom stir-fry sauce, which is the plant-based equivalent of oyster sauce and can be used as a substitute.

## SOY SAUCE

This staple is possibly the most-used ingredient in my cooking, and probably the same goes for many other Asian chefs, too. You'll find soy sauce in almost every recipe in this book. I like to stock up on both classic light and dark soy sauces.

My go-to brands are Lee Kum Kee or Amoy. Both are large, well-known and established household brands in the Chinese market. The Thai brand, Healthy Boy, is also a great alternative, as is the Japanese Kikkoman.

The difference between each brand and type of soy sauce can get pretty complicated if you dig into their story and methods of production. On a basic level, it's usually the type of soybean used, the way it is brewed and for how long, but I'd say keep it simple and stick to the classic types, especially if you're a beginner to Asian-style cooking. If you can, try to avoid non-Asian brands as they don't tend to be as authentic or use traditional production methods. You may also come across bottles labelled as "first extract" or "premium". Think of "first extract" as the equivalent of "extra virgin" in olive oil – it is of the highest quality.

You will also find various options when it comes to the level of sodium in different soy sauces, which you are welcome to choose based on your preference and/or for health-related reasons. For those who are gluten intolerant, soy sauce can be replaced with coconut aminos, which is soy-, wheat- and gluten-free.

## HOISIN SAUCE

Made from fermented soybean paste with added spices, hoisin sauce is commonly used in stir-fries and as a marinade. It is vegan and brings a combination of tangy and sweet flavours, with a hint of spice.

If you've ever had Peking duck, you may recall it being served with a sweet dark brown sauce – that's most likely to have been hoisin sauce. You may also have had duck spring rolls served with hoisin as well. Basically, it is delicious as a condiment as well as an ingredient.

## SESAME OIL

In much the same way as olive oil is used in Italian cooking, sesame oil is a popular staple in Chinese cuisine. However, unlike olive oil, you need to go easy when using sesame oil as it has a stronger flavour profile and can dominate a dish if not used in moderation. When used in the right way, the flavour and aroma of sesame oil can elevate a dish; start with a teaspoon at a time and taste as you go. Please note that all mentions of sesame oil in this book refer to "toasted sesame oil", which may be labelled "pure sesame oil" if buying brands such as Lee Kum Kee or Kadoya. Regular sesame oil made with untoasted seeds is lighter in colour and has a more subtle, nutty flavour profile.

Toasted sesame oil is unsuitable for frying over a high heat, unlike sunflower oil or rapeseed oil, as it has a low-smoke point, which makes it unstable. I tend to use sesame oil in sauces or add it towards the end of cooking for a nutty taste and aroma.

## CHILLI OIL

-------------------------------------------

I should mention that I *love* all kinds of chilli (chile) oil – my motto when cooking is "if in doubt, add chilli oil". The vibrant colour and punch of flavour it brings to a dish is unmatched by any other condiment.

There are so many different kinds of chilli oil to choose from, so I always stock a few types in my kitchen. They range from ones with Sichuan peppercorns to those flavoured with dried shrimp, and each jar has its own place in my heart. I don't like to stick to just one as I prefer to pick and pair my chilli oils with whatever I'm cooking, and that usually depends on the main ingredients in the recipe. So, for dishes that are seafood based, I'd use one with dried shrimp to enhance the seafood umami, rather than go for the more unique flavour of Sichuan peppercorns.

If you want to make your own, I have also included my own recipes (see p.23 and 24) for you to try at home.

## CHILLIES & CHILLI FLAKES

-------------------------------------------

The Sichuan chilli (chile), with its interesting alternative name "facing heaven chilli" (朝天椒) is commonly used in Chinese cuisine, specifically in Sichuan cooking. Often available to buy dried in bags, the deep-red chillies, make a perfect mildly spiced oil with a bright red colour.

Being mild in heat, Sichuan chillies can be used in almost anything. To incorporate into cooking, I like to cut the chilli into pieces, remove the seeds and add to stir-fries, or use to make chilli oils (see p.24). They are commonly paired with Sichuan peppercorns to create dishes that are *mala*, aka "numbing spice", which you will come across in several recipes in this book.

Another favourite and one of the most important ingredients in Korean cooking is gochugaru or Korean red pepper. It is used in kimchi, stews, marinades, broths and chilli oil. I always have a small tub of the hot pepper flakes to hand, but you can also find gochugaru in powdered form.

The spice level of gochugaru is moderate with a hint of smoky sweetness. I don't recommend substituting gochugaru chilli flakes or powder with another type of chilli powder, such as cayenne pepper, since the potency and flavour do differ. Do seek out gochugaru in your local Asian grocer, if you can – it's worth trying.

## FISH SAUCE

-------------------------------------------

A staple ingredient in Thai and Vietnamese food, fish sauce is not usually used in Chinese cooking. It may smell funky when you catch a whiff of it straight from the bottle, but a splash adds so much flavour and umami to cooking that it's definitely worth having a bottle of the sauce handy in your kitchen. Just trust me on this!

My favourite, and one recommended by many Thai and Vietnamese friends and chefs, is the Tiparos brand. But, if more convenient, you can usually find the Squid brand in major supermarkets in the world food aisle as well as in Asian grocers. The main difference between the two is the level of sweetness. Try both for yourself and decide!

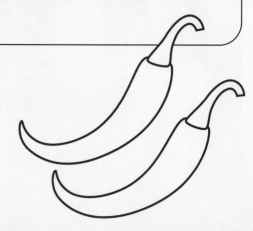

## RICE VINEGAR

In Chinese cooking, white rice vinegar, sometimes known as rice wine vinegar, is more subtle in terms of flavour and acidity to other types, such as malt or white distilled vinegar. I particularly like to use it in sauces to add a dash of acidity and to balance out flavours. Dishes with a rich flavour or slightly higher fat content, such as Honey Garlic Chicken (see p.118), also benefit from the tang vinegar brings. Apple cider vinegar or lemon juice make good alternatives.

Chinese black vinegar, otherwise known as Chinkiang vinegar, is made from glutinous rice and has a distinct and full flavour. A little goes a long way, so add it a bit at a time and taste as you go to avoid overpowering a dish. My favourite way to use it is in sauces and dips, namely my Ultimate Dumpling Sauce (see p.26) and also in Vegan Dan Dan Noodles (see p.108). Although they may look similar, I wouldn't recommend substituting balsamic vinegar for Chinese black vinegar, as it tastes very different and is sweeter, being made from fermented grape juice.

## MISO PASTE

Japanese miso paste is an ingredient I always have in the fridge, just like Korean gochujang. I love how versatile it is and the umami flavour it brings to a dish. I'm sure you've seen many fusion dishes using miso in restaurants and recipes, and just like its Korean cousin, gochujang, do try it in recipes where you need extra savouriness and flavour – it works wonders!

You commonly find white, brown and red miso in supermarkets and Asian food stores. The difference in colour comes from the way the soybeans are fermented, whether it's with white or brown rice or other grains, such as barley, as well as the length of the fermentation process. In terms of flavour, when choosing a miso paste to cook with, I prefer white miso as it has a more subtle flavour, yet becomes stronger the more that is added. It's worth experimenting with different types.

## CHILLI PASTES

I always have a tub of Korean gochujang paste at home. The fermented chilli paste is made from the same type of chilli as gochugaru (see left), but using a different method of production. This staple Korean ingredient is deep red in colour and has a rich, sweet, umami flavour. I like to use it in several classic dishes, such as Korean Beef Bulgogi (see p.164) and Kimchi Tofu Stew (p.94).

Chinese chilli bean paste (doubanjiang) is made from a combination of preserved chilli peppers, soy beans and broad bean paste. The result is a pungent and spicy Sichuan-style condiment used in dishes such as Fish-Fragrant Aubergine (p.88) and Sichuan Dry Pot Potatoes (p.112) – a little of the paste goes a long way.

GOCHUJANG

RED MISO

CHILLI OIL

DOUBANJIANG

WHITE MISO

## CHINESE COOKING WINE

-------------------------------------------

Also known as Shaoxing wine (绍兴酒), due to its place of origin (a city in Zhejiang Province), this cooking wine is a staple in many authentic Chinese dishes. When I was at university, I didn't bother investing in a bottle (it was five pounds and for me that was precious money I could use to buy actual wine). It was only relatively recently that I added it to my cooking must-haves and realized the difference it makes to my cooking.

The ancient amber-coloured cooking wine adds a complexity of flavour to a dish when used in cooking or in a marinade. Its alcohol content helps to tenderize meat and improve the marinating process; it works by bonding with the water and fat in the meat, helping the flavours bind with, and absorb into, the protein more effectively.

Science aside, when I first started using Chinese cooking wine, I learned the hard way that it needs to be added in small amounts as otherwise its flavour will dominate a dish. It is particularly great in braised dishes, such as my Red Braised Pork Belly (see p.110) and seafood dishes, like the Steamed Scallops with Glass Noodles (see p.126) and Crispy Sea Bass (see p.142).

Given that it is around 14 per cent abv, if you're looking for a substitute that is alcohol-free, a good-quality vegetable or chicken stock can be used instead. Admittedly, sometimes if I've run out of my Shaoxing wine supply and the recipe only needs a splash, I'll just leave it out.

## MIRIN

-------------------------------------------

Commonly used in Japanese cooking, mirin is a type of rice wine, but with a lower alcohol content and sweeter taste than sake - 14 per cent versus 20 per cent abv, respectively. The sugar content comes from the fermenting rice, rather than added.

I first came across the sweet rice wine in a teriyaki chicken recipe before I realized it is used in almost everything in Japanese cuisine, including rice bowls and sushi. When used in a marinade for meat, the alcohol in the mirin helps to tenderize it as well as add a subtle sweetness and glossy appearance when it is cooked. In addition, in the same way Chinese cooking wine is added to mask the slight "fishiness" of seafood, mirin can also do the same.

If you prefer to cook without alcohol, there is an alcohol-free version that can be found at Japanese food stores. Otherwise, I would recommend making a sugar syrup with granulated sugar – about 1:3 sugar to water ratio.

## MONOSODIUM GLUTAMATE (MSG)

- - - - - - - - - - - - - - - - - - - - - - - - - - - - - - - - - - - - - -

A popular flavour enhancer and seasoning, monosodium glutamate (MSG) is added to soups, sauces and processed meats, yet you may be surprised to learn that it also naturally occurs in foods, such as tomatoes and Parmesan cheese. Despite the controversy around the use of MSG, it is what creates the fifth taste or umami, after sweet, salty, sour and bitter. This is down to an amino acid called glutamate, which activates our taste receptors to the sensation of "deliciousness".

It has been known for some time in Japan that boiling dried kombu seaweed to make dashi is key to making a delicious broth. The same can be said for dried shrimp or bonito flakes or fermented soy. Yet, it wasn't until the early 1900s when a Japanese chemist, Kikunae Ikeda, isolated glutamate from kombu seaweed and added ordinary salt (sodium) to create what is now known as monosodium glutamate. At this point, MSG became more cost-friendly and easily accessible to you and me.

A few decades ago, it was common belief that MSG should be avoided for health reasons. Yet, countless studies have proven that it is nothing but safe for consumption. Just like sugar, salt, fat, you name it, when consumed in sensible amounts, MSG does not contribute or come with increased health risks. That said, if the caution towards MSG stems from allergy issues, then sure, please do skip it in your cooking and meals. Otherwise, MSG can be a great substitute for table salt as it contains less sodium per gram, while still adding flavour to dishes.

## PEANUT BUTTER

- - - - - - - - - - - - - - - - - - - - - - - - - - - - - - - - -

Technically, Chinese cuisine favours sesame paste, but given it's not a readily available ingredient, I prefer to substitute it with peanut butter, thanks to its distinct nutty flavour.

While tahini is also a sesame paste, the way it is typically produced (the use of raw, hulled sesame as opposed to toasted sesame seeds in Chinese sesame pastes) means it has a very different flavour profile. This is why I don't usually recommend substituting with tahini - that said, if you have a peanut allergy, tahini would be a great option!

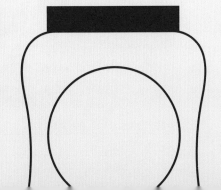

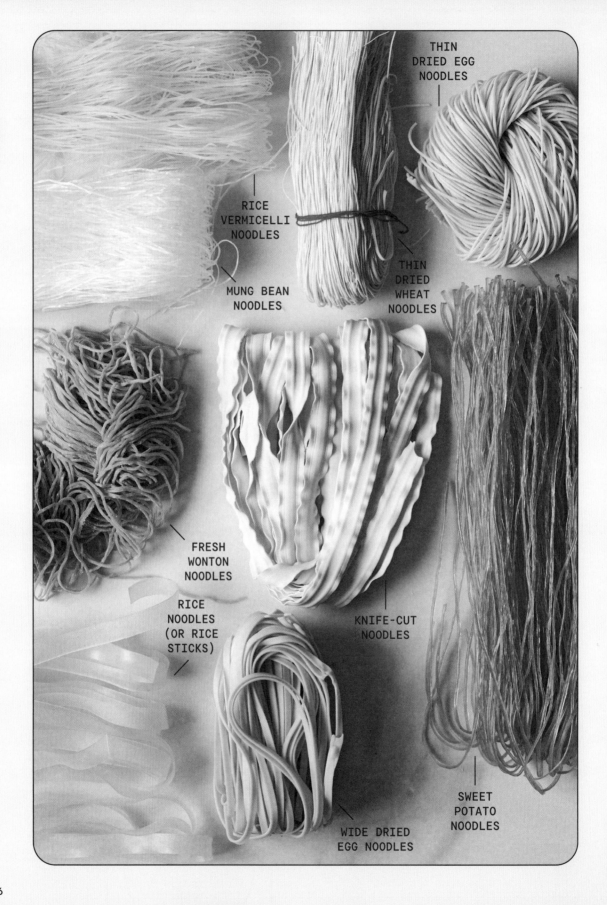

RICE
VERMICELLI
NOODLES

THIN
DRIED EGG
NOODLES

MUNG BEAN
NOODLES

THIN
DRIED
WHEAT
NOODLES

FRESH
WONTON
NOODLES

RICE
NOODLES
(OR RICE
STICKS)

KNIFE-CUT
NOODLES

WIDE DRIED
EGG NOODLES

SWEET
POTATO
NOODLES

## DRIED NOODLES

Dried wheat noodles are my go-to as I like how versatile they are. They also come in many aesthetically pleasing shapes, such as traditional knife-cut noodles. These, as the name suggests, are wheat noodles that are hand-cut into ribbons with a knife, rather than a machine. They have a slightly chewy texture and not only look pretty, but also catch and hold whatever sauce you toss them with. You can, make fresh knife-cut noodles from scratch, but given how great the dried ones are, I recommend you seek them out. Find them in large Asian grocers or online.

Japanese ramen noodles are probably one of the most popular types of thin wheat noodle. Traditionally, ramen noodles are made with an alkaline ingredient called *kansui*, which gives them a yellowish tinge and curly appearance. Fresh ramen noodles require a lot of effort to make so the instant dried ramen nests are a great alternative.

Egg noodles are also a common type of noodle to be found in a variety of shapes and sizes. I like to use them for stir-fries as they hold their shape well.

Rice and glass (cellophane) noodles are a great alternative to wheat noodles for those who are intolerant or allergic to gluten. These include mung bean noodles, commonly described as vermicelli noodles, since they are much thinner than wheat or egg noodles. They also become a translucent white colour when dried. Sweet potato noodles, on the other hand, are thicker and a darker shade of translucent grey when uncooked. Once boiled, these noodles turn glassy in appearance. Look for them in recipes such as Japchae (see p.98) and in Steamed Scallops with Glass Noodles (see p.126). To prepare, I like to soak glass noodles in hot water for around 5 minutes to soften. Once softened, they don't require more than a couple of minutes to prevent them overcooking. Their bouncy texture is what I, and many others, love about them.

## FRESH NOODLES

Fresh, thick wheat udon noodles are chewy when cooked and can usually be bought in vacuum-packed pouches. They are my go-to when I want udon noodles as they are portioned into individual packets and are conveniently ready-to-use.

Fresh egg noodles have more of a bite than dried egg noodles. My favourite are fresh wonton noodles, which, as the name suggests, are great in wonton noodle soups.

## RICE

My go-to rice for day-to-day meals is short-grain Japanese rice. I personally love its texture and slight natural sweetness. Also sold as sushi rice, this type of short-grain white rice is fluffy and slightly sticky when cooked, but don't confuse it with sticky rice, which is more accurately named as glutinous rice. The texture of short-grain Japanese rice is firmer and chewy when cooked. When uncooked, the rice grains are plumper than Thai jasmine rice, for instance.

Thai jasmine rice is another type that I stock up on at home. This fragrant long-grain rice is commonly found in southeast Asia and I usually pair it with dishes, such as Spicy Thai Basil Pork (see p.156) as well as non-Thai dishes, including Hainanese Chicken Rice (see p.160). When cooked, jasmine rice has a subtle pandan-like fragrance that I love. It is more fluffy than Japanese rice, and the texture of the grains is softer too, so they slightly stick together, making them easy to scoop up with chopsticks and eat in one mouthful.

# The Small

# Bits

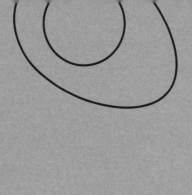

Before we dive into the dishes and recipes that have carried me through my life, let me introduce you to a few essentials that you'll find mentioned throughout the recipes. Think of them as the small but nevertheless important characters in a book – the vital ones that bring the storyline together.

An honourable mention goes to three of my favourite sauces. When I first started cooking, I never really delved into learning how to make condiments as they seemed such a small part of a dish. As time went on, I realized that the difference between two very similar recipes is often the sauce that they come with – and it can influence the success, or not, of a dish.

To me, chilli (chile) oil can bring so much life and character to a dish. The red oil and hue it adds can also make a plate of food that much more appetizing visually. Homemade is best, so I've attached two variations of my go-to recipes, which are both customizable.

For those who prefer a sauce without chilli, a humble ginger and spring onion (green onion) one is also great. I love this sauce on top of steamed or poached chicken and it can add so much umami to a plain and simple meal.

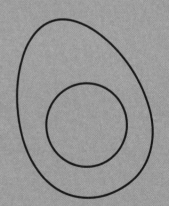

Finally, I have to mention the ultimate dumpling sauce. No dumpling is complete without a little dipping sauce on the side, and "what's in the sauce?" is one of the most frequently asked questions whenever I post an image or video of my dumplings on social media. You can find out on page 26.

Of course, the important bits don't just stop at sauces. You'll also see in this book that I love adding a side of pickles. Why? Because the acidity, freshness and crunch they bring to a dish is immeasurable. They can also serve as a palate cleanser, enabling you to distinguish between different flavours.

But, there's no better way to start than with that essential Asian accompaniment – rice, and my go-to's are short-grain Japanese and Thai jasmine (see p.17). I show you how to cook the perfect fluffy rice, and there's no need for a rice cooker.

# Steamed Rice
## (without a rice cooker)

**PREP:**
10 MINS

**COOK:**
20 MINS

You may be thinking what on earth is a recipe for steamed rice doing in this book? Well, truth be told, I haven't always had a rice cooker on hand to cook perfect rice. During my days at university, aside from living mainly on noodles because it was way easier, I made do with a conventional saucepan whenever I cooked rice.

This book features lots of recipes where I suggest serving the dish with steamed rice. So, if you're not sure how best to make the perfect steamed rice without a rice cooker, let me help you. That way you avoid buying microwave pouches of rice and can make it fresh and perfectly, at home every time.

In my experience, the key is to use the same cup to measure both your rice and the water; this means, you can use a mug to measure the rice as long as you use the same mug to measure your water. The ratio of rice to water when using a rice cooker is usually 1:1, but if you're cooking it on the stove, you'll need a little more water, about 1:1.2 ratio of rice to water, which usually amounts to a few extra tablespoons.

---

- 275g (generous 1½ cups) rice, preferably Japanese short-grain or Thai jasmine rice

Wash the rice thoroughly in a sieve under cold running water to remove the excess starch on the outside of the grains.

Place the washed rice in a pan and add 350ml (1½ cups) of water to cover. Add an extra tablespoon or two of water to cover the rice, if needed.

Bring the water to a gentle boil on the stove, then turn the heat down to the lowest setting. Cover with the lid and simmer for about 15 minutes, or until the water is absorbed by the rice and the grains are tender. Check to make sure the rice is fully cooked. If not, add an extra 2–3 tablespoons of water, then return the pan to a low heat and steam the rice, covered with the lid, for a bit longer until tender and the water has been absorbed.

Turn the heat off and let the rice sit in the pan, with the lid on, for another 5 minutes. Remove the lid and fluff up the rice with a fork. Serve the steamed rice with your choice of dish or as mentioned in the recipe.

EASY
CHILLI
OIL

SICHUAN
CHILLI
OIL

THE
ULTIMATE
DUMPLING
SAUCE

GINGER
& SPRING
ONION
SAUCE

# Easy Chilli Oil

This is a must-have in my kitchen - the humble chilli (chile) oil. You can absolutely pick up a good one in Asian supermarkets, but I do love making a fresh batch at home. Not only does it make my kitchen smell amazing, it tastes better than shop-bought, and can easily be customized to suit my own taste preferences, as it can yours, too.

In this book, I've included two chilli oil recipes. This one uses very few ingredients, mostly things you'd commonly find without too much trouble. If you want something with a bit more spice and heat, try my Sichuan Chilli Oil on the following page.

---

- 2 tbsp garlic powder
- 5 tbsp dried Sichuan chilli (chile) flakes (see p.12)
- 2 tbsp white sesame seeds
- ½ tsp salt
- 1 tsp granulated sugar
- pinch of MSG, optional
- 250ml (1 cup plus 1 tbsp) cooking oil of choice, such as vegetable or sunflower oil
- 1 bay leaf

Place the garlic powder, chilli flakes, sesame seeds, salt, sugar and MSG, if using, in a sterilized heatproof jar or bowl, large enough to hold the oil and flavourings.

Place the oil and bay leaf in a small saucepan and heat to around 185°C (365°F). If you do not have a kitchen thermometer, heat the oil until small bubbles appear on the surface. Switch off the heat and let the oil sit for 2 minutes to cool off slightly and to avoid scorching the chillies.

Carefully pour the hot oil into the jar or bowl. The oil will sizzle as you pour it in, "cooking" the contents. Stir a few times to mix and let the oil cool completely. Put the lid on the jar, if using.

The chilli oil is ready to use straightaway but the flavours will intensify over the next 24 hours, if left.

Spoon the oil into the jar, if using, cover with the lid and store in a cool, dark place. Refrigerate once opened and use within 3 months.

# Sichuan Chilli Oil

 四 川 辣 椒 油

● PREP:
5 MINS

● COOK:
15 MINS

● STORE:
UP TO 3
MONTHS

Following on from my recipe for Easy Chilli Oil (see p.23), it's time to spice things up with my Sichuan version. What makes it special is the addition of the number one spice - Sichuan pepper. If you don't like its characteristic numbing sensation and flavour, you can leave it out and just use the rest of the spices, it will still taste great.

---

### FLAVOURINGS FOR THE JAR/BOWL
--------------------------------

- 6-8 tbsp dried Sichuan chilli flakes (alternatively, use gochugaru, see p.12)
- 1 tsp salt
- 1 tsp granulated sugar
- 1 tbsp white sesame seeds
- 1 tbsp Chinese black vinegar
- pinch of MSG, optional

### SPICES FOR TOASTING
--------------------------------

- 1 star anise
- 1 cinnamon stick
- 1 tbsp Sichuan peppercorns
- 1 bay leaf

### FOR THE OIL & INFUSION
--------------------------------

- 250ml (1 cup plus 1 tbsp) cooking oil of choice, such as vegetable or sunflower oil
- 3-4 garlic cloves, smashed and peeled
- 3-4 slices fresh root ginger (don't slice it too thinly or it may burn)

Add all the flavourings to a sterilized heatproof jar or bowl, large enough to hold the oil and flavourings.

Heat a small pan on a medium heat and add the spices for toasting. Allow the spices to gently toast for around 2–3 minutes, shaking the pan occasionally to prevent them burning.

Now, add the oil and infusion ingredients to the pan. Let the oil warm and bubble away gently on a medium–low heat, taking care not to burn the garlic or otherwise it will introduce a bitter flavour. Once the garlic and ginger have turned golden brown, about 4–5 minutes, turn the heat off and remove the pan from the stove. The temperature of the oil should be around 185°C (365°F) at this point.

Carefully, strain the oil into a jug and discard the contents of the strainer. Set aside for a few minutes to let the oil cool down slightly.

Now, carefully pour the strained oil into the jar or bowl containing the flavourings. The oil will sizzle as you pour it in, "cooking" the contents. Stir a few times to mix and let the oil cool completely. Put the lid on the jar, if using.

The Sichuan chilli oil is ready to use straightaway, but the flavours will intensify over the next 24 hours if left.

Spoon the oil into the jar, if using, cover with the lid and store in a cool, dark place. Refrigerate once opened and use within 3 months.

# Ginger & Spring Onion Sauce

PREP:
10 MINS

COOK:
5 MINS

STORE:
UP TO
2 WEEKS

For the folks who are looking for a non-spicy condiment after two chilli (chile) oil recipes, this one's for you. It may sound simple, yet ginger, garlic and spring onion (green onion) form the foundation of Chinese cooking, and it would be hard to find a dish that does not feature at least one of these ingredients, if not all three. This simple combination is delicious and perfect with so many dishes, such as bowls of rice, grilled chicken or other white meat, cold noodles and more.

I prefer the cooked version of this sauce as opposed to the raw, since the hot oil helps to extract more of the flavour from the aromatics, but if you're in a hurry, you can definitely make this with cold oil - it's worth trying both options to see which one you prefer.

---

- 120ml (½ cup) cooking oil of choice, such as vegetable or sunflower oil
- 50g (1¾oz) fresh root ginger, peeled and minced
- 3 garlic cloves, finely chopped
- 100g (3½oz) spring onions (green onions), finely chopped, white and green parts separated
- ½ tsp salt
- pinch of sugar
- pinch of MSG, optional

### PAIRING SUGGESTIONS
------------------------------------

- Hainanese Chicken Rice (see p.160)
- Pork & Leek Sheng Jian Baos (see p.190)

Warm the cooking oil in a small saucepan on a medium–high heat (when you carefully hover your hand over the pan you should be able to feel warmth coming from the oil).

Add the ginger to the pan and cook for 1 minute, stirring, then add the garlic and the white part of the spring onions. Stir to mix and cook for another minute.

Stir in the green part of the spring onions and cook for another minute. At this point, the oil should be gently sizzling and your kitchen should smell great.

Remove the pan from the heat and season with the salt, sugar and MSG, if using. Taste and adjust the seasoning, if needed.

Carefully pour the hot oil into a sterilized heatproof jar or bowl, large enough to hold the oil and flavourings.

The sauce is ready to serve straightaway or store in the fridge in the lidded jar for up to 2 weeks.

# The Ultimate Dumpling Sauce

● PREP:
5 MINS

One of the most frequently asked questions whenever I post pictures and recipes of dumplings on social media is, "what's that sauce you've got there?". I've never really considered the sauce as a recipe worth sharing before, as far as I can remember it has always been a bit of a freestyle thing. But looking back, I guess I do have a go-to combination of ingredients that I love to enjoy with freshly made dumplings, particularly pan-fried ones with a crispy bottom. So, here it is.

---

- 2 tbsp Chinese black vinegar
- 1 tbsp light soy sauce
- ½ tbsp sesame oil
- 1 tbsp finely chopped fresh coriander (cilantro)
- 1 tbsp finely chopped spring onions (green onions)
- 1 tbsp Easy Chilli Oil (see p.23), optional

PAIRING SUGGESTION
--------------------------------
- Dumpling and Wonton recipes (see pp.184-203)

Mix all the ingredients for the dipping sauce together in a bowl, adding the chilli oil if you like.

Pour the sauce into small bowls and serve alongside your dumplings and wontons.

# Pickled Cucumber

醋溜小黄瓜

●
PREP:
15 MINS

One of the first non-sauce recipes in the book, and undoubtedly one of the simplest, although that doesn't mean this pickle is any less tasty than the other recipes! I love accompanying many of my dishes, especially the ones with big, bold flavours, with this tangy pickled cucumber. It instantly brings a level of freshness, and balances out anything rich or spicy.

- 1 whole cucumber, ends trimmed, about 250-300g (9-10oz)
- 2 tbsp rice vinegar or apple cider vinegar, or fresh lemon juice
- 1 tsp granulated sugar
- ¼ tsp salt

## PAIRING SUGGESTIONS
---------------------------------

- Easy Braised Pork Ribs (see p.66)
- Hainanese Chicken Rice (see p.160)

Using a vegetable peeler, peel the cucumber lengthways into long ribbons. The first one or two strips may be the green outer skin that you'll want to discard, stop when you get to the seedy part in the middle.

Place the vinegar, sugar and salt in a large bowl and mix together until the sugar dissolves. Add the cucumber ribbons, stir gently until combined, then leave to stand for 5–10 minutes before serving. The pickle is best eaten within a few hours of making, since it begins to discolour and turn yellow if left for too long.

Serve as an accompaniment to many dishes in this book, including Chinese-style braised pork ribs and Hainanese chicken rice.

# Pickled Carrot & Daikon

**PREP:**
15 MINS

**STORE:**
UP TO
1 WEEK

This is another one of my favourite pickles, especially with dishes that are slightly fatty or rich. The method is very similar to the Pickled Cucumber (see p.27), the main difference being that the carrot and daikon take a bit longer to pickle, around 2-3 hours, but you can leave it for up to 24 hours. It is a pickle that is more commonly used in Vietnamese cooking, rather than Chinese, but as a lover of fusion food and bringing the best of both together, I wanted to make sure it featured in this book.

---

- 3 carrots, peeled, about 200g (7oz) total weight
- 200g (7oz) daikon radish, peeled
- 200ml (scant 1 cup) hot water
- 50g (¼ cup) granulated sugar
- 60ml (4 tbsp) rice vinegar
- ½ tsp salt

### PAIRING SUGGESTIONS
---------------------------------

- Beijing Zhajiangmian (see p.140)
- Spicy Thai Basil Pork (see p.156)

Prepare the carrots and daikon by slicing the vegetables lengthways with a mandolin, then cutting them into thin matchsticks. Alternatively, use a julienne peeler. Set aside briefly.

In a large heatproof bowl, mix the hot water with the sugar, rice vinegar and salt. Stir until the sugar dissolves, then leave to cool.

Place the vegetables in the bowl and mix to ensure they are submerged in the pickling liquid. Cover and leave to macerate at room temperature for at least 2-3 hours. The pickle can be left for up to 24 hours. You may wish to taste the pickle every 6 hours or so to check the level of acidity, according to your preference.

Decant the pickle into a clean sterilized jar for easy storage, cover with a lid and keep in the fridge. The pickle is best eaten within 1 week and can be served as an accompaniment to many dishes, such as Beijing zhajianmian or spicy Thai basil pork.

PICKLED
CARROT
& DAIKON

PICKLED
CUCUMBER

# Japanese Soy–Marinated Eggs

日式溏心蛋

**PREP:** **COOK:**
**10 MINS*** **10 MINS****

*plus marinating
**store up to 3 days

Eggs are one of my favourite foods in the world. They're versatile and delicious and can be cooked in a multitude of ways. These soy-marinated eggs, with their jammy centre, are commonly served as part of a ramen, but they're also super tasty on their own or on top of rice. You can make a few and store them in the fridge for up to 2–3 days. Try not to marinate them for longer than 3 days as the yolks harden a little and take on a texture similar to a cured egg, losing their lovely "jamminess".

---

- 1 tbsp rice vinegar or any white vinegar
- 6 eggs, at room temperature
- 75ml (5 tbsp) light soy sauce
- 3 tbsp mirin
- Steamed Rice (see p.21), to serve

**PAIRING SUGGESTION**
---------------------------------
- Spiced Lamb Soup Noodles (see p.148)
- Chilli & Lime Salmon Rice Bowl (see p.81)

Bring a small saucepan of water to the boil, then turn down the heat slightly. Add the vinegar and gently lower the eggs into the pan with the help of a spoon (the vinegar will help the eggs peel more easily once boiled). Cook the eggs at a gentle boil for 7 minutes.

While the eggs are cooking, combine the soy sauce and mirin in a jug with 150ml (⅔ cup) of water to make a marinade.

Once the eggs are ready, remove with a slotted spoon and immediately place in a bowl of iced water. Leave for 4–5 minutes before carefully peeling.

Place the peeled eggs in a ziplock bag and pour in the marinade. Squeeze out as much air as possible before sealing the bag shut. Leave to marinate in the refrigerator for at least 3–4 hours. Store the eggs in the marinade in a lidded container and eat within 3 days.

Serve the eggs on top of steamed rice, or add to a bowl of warm spiced lamb soup noodles.

# Chinese Tea Eggs

**PREP:**
**10 MINS***

**COOK:**
**10 MINS**

*plus marinating

These are a common sight in convenience stores and snack kiosks in train stations throughout China - you can smell their fragrant tea aroma a mile off. Usually, tea eggs are cooked for so long that the yolks become dry and typically have a grey tinge around the yolk, which is not as enjoyable as this version - I'm definitely a jammy yolk kind of girl. So, instead of overboiling the eggs, these are prepared in a similar way to the Japanese Soy-Marinated Eggs (see p.31), but the flavour profile is more complex with the addition of spices and black tea. Use Chinese cinnamon (cassia) here, and not Ceylon cinnamon. The former has a preferable stronger, slightly bitter flavour, and looks different too - the stick has a hollow appearance and resembles a piece of tree bark.

- 6 eggs, at room temperature
- 4 tbsp light soy sauce
- 2 tbsp dark soy sauce
- 3 tbsp mirin
- 1 small stick Chinese cinnamon (cassia), about 5cm (2in) long
- ½ tbsp Sichuan pepper
- 1 star anise
- 1 bay leaf
- 2 black tea bags

**PAIRING SUGGESTIONS**

- Beijing Zhajiangmian (see p.140)
- Wonton Noodle Soup (see p.202)

Bring a small saucepan of water to the boil, then turn down the heat slightly. Gently lower the eggs into the pan using a spoon and cook the eggs at a gentle boil for 7 minutes. If you'd like a firmer yolk, cook the eggs for 1–2 minutes more. Once the eggs are ready, remove with a slotted spoon and immediately place in a bowl of iced water. Leave to cool for 4–5 minutes.

While the eggs are cooling, combine 250ml (1 cup plus 1 tablespoon) of water with both types of soy sauce, the mirin, spices and bay leaf in the pan. Bring to a gentle simmer and add the tea bags. Simmer for 4–5 minutes, until the liquid is infused with the flavourings. Remove from the heat, strain discarding the solids, and allow the marinade to cool completely.

Do not peel the eggs but gently crack the shells all over with the back of a teaspoon (this will give the eggs a marbled pattern after marinating). Pour the cooled marinade into a ziplock bag and add the eggs. Squeeze out as much air as possible before sealing the bag. Leave to marinate in the refrigerator for at least 3 hours, preferably overnight.

To serve, peel the eggs. They can be enjoyed at room temperature as a snack or serve as an accompaniment to Beijing zhajiangmian or wonton noodle soup.

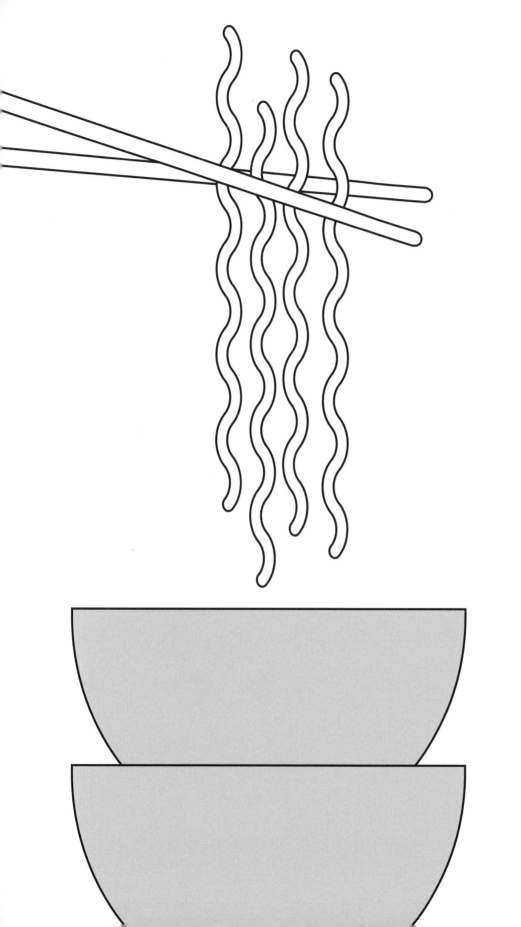

# Simplicity

# &

# Peace

# Simplicity & Peace

Looking back
now, many of my
favourite and most
loved dishes came
from my childhood.

I lived in Shanghai until my parents' divorce when I was aged seven. The three of us resided in a small one-bed apartment on the seventh and top floor of a block, in and amongst many other similar-looking blocks in a large residential village near to Tongji University, where both my parents worked.

My school, Tongji Elementary, was a five-minute walk away so from a young age, I don't remember when exactly, I would walk myself to school and back every day. On the odd occasion I'd stop off to see my mum at the university to study in her office while she worked. It was very safe to walk around by yourself, even as a child, and despite it being a large neighbourhood, lots of people knew each other and it was impossible to walk without bumping into a familiar face.

My mum and dad had very opposing personalities, which I never fully understood until I became an adult. My mum loved to go on about things and my dad was not a talker. They both had their strong opinions and beliefs about certain subjects, but it wasn't until I became older did I fully understand why they were destined to split up. That said, despite them arguing relentlessly as I grew up, the kitchen was always a place of peace. Arguments never took place there, probably because my dad was not a cook, so he steered well clear of the kitchen; he was also bound to be wrong if he landed a foot in there.

The meals I ate back then were mostly cooked by my mum, and she had a strong preference for food that was simple and made with only a few ingredients. She's always been into Chinese medicine and its philosophy, so it was usual for her to inform us

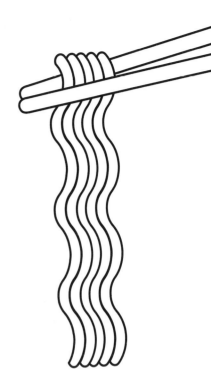

how nutritious her cooking was. She loved to explain which foods were particularly rich in certain vitamins and minerals, like how tomatoes were great for the skin due to their antioxidant content, while eggs would help me grow thanks to the significant amount of protein and minerals they would provide. So, it should come as no surprise to learn that the classic Tomato & Egg Stir-Fry (see p.48) often frequented our family dinner table, given how delicious and nutritious it was – and still is.

I never really appreciated Mum's cooking as a child until I left her side after my parents separated. Back then her meals seemed predictable and unadventurous. A typical dinner for the three of us would be made up of something like a braised meat dish, alongside two vegetable stir fries and, of course, three bowls of steamed rice. Looking back now, many of my favourite and most loved dishes came from my childhood. They are those that are simple and uncomplicated because they showcase the flavour of the ingredients, without heavy sauces and long cooking times.

The recipes in this chapter are exactly that. You won't need to venture far to find the right ingredients, since I like to use items that are easily found in your local supermarket – eggs, wheat noodles, garlic, peanut butter, and so on. These reliable staple ingredients, which are used in my Creamy 10-Minute Peanut Noodles (see p.45), Easy Braised Pork Ribs (see p.66), and Smacked Cucumber (see p.40) are also what got me through many busy university days and hectic work weeks. Knowing that I'll be able to tuck into something I've always loved in next to no time just makes me feel instantly at ease. So, let's begin...

# Egg Drop Soup

**PREP:**
5 MINS

**COOK:**
5 MINS

This may be called egg drop soup, but the literal Chinese translation is *egg flower soup*. The name comes from the way the egg swirls round the bowl, looking like little flower petals, when poured into the hot broth or water. Doesn't that sound so pretty?

And what better dish to open the first recipe chapter than this simple and delicious soup, which forms the foundation of many Chinese soups, including variations with seaweed, corn or tomato. You can customize the soup freely to make it your own, but since the basic version is one of my personal faves, let's start here.

- 500ml (generous 2 cups) good-quality chicken stock (homemade is best)
- ½ tsp sesame oil
- ½ tsp salt
- ¼ tsp ground white pepper
- 1 tbsp cornflour (cornstarch)
- 1 large egg, whisked
- 1 handful of chopped spring onions (green onions)

**PAIRING SUGGESTIONS**

- - - - - - - - - - - - - - - - - - - - - - - - - - - - - - - - -

- Shanghai Spring Onion Oil Noodles (see p.42)
- Easy Braised Pork Ribs (see p.66)

Heat the chicken broth in a saucepan on a medium heat and season with the sesame oil, salt and white pepper. Mix to combine and adjust the seasoning to taste.

Mix the cornflour with 3 tablespoons of water in a small bowl and stir until evenly combined. Pour the mixture into the pan and stir until the soup thickens slightly and has warmed up.

Gently swirl the soup with a spoon and gradually pour in the whisked egg. Allow the egg to swirl around for a few seconds before stirring the broth – this will allow the egg to form into separate strands.

Toss in the spring onions, then ladle the soup into two serving bowls and enjoy as a starter to Shanghai spring onion oil noodles and easy braised pork ribs, or your own choice of dish – the soup is very versatile.

# Smacked Cucumber

●
PREP:
10 MINS

Confession: growing up I never liked cucumber. It was one of my least favourite vegetables, and I found it watery and lacking in any distinguishing flavour. In short, I thought it was boring.

Enter the tongue-tingling Chinese side dish of smacked cucumber, which over time has become one of my favourite ways to eat the vegetable. This is a perfectly refreshing accompaniment to almost any dish in this book. I love pairing it with my juicy Chinese five-spice chicken, so you should definitely make that too while you're at it!

- 1 whole cucumber or 300g (10oz) baby cucumbers
- ½ tbsp light soy sauce
- 1 tbsp Chinese black vinegar
- 1 tsp sesame oil
- 3 garlic cloves, minced
- 1 tsp granulated sugar
- ½ tsp salt
- 1 tbsp Easy Chilli Oil (see p.23), or adjust to suit personal preference
- 1 tsp toasted sesame seeds
- 1 small handful of thinly sliced spring onions (green onions)

PAIRING SUGGESTIONS
- - - - - - - - - - - - - - - - - - - - - - - - - -

- Chinese Five-Spice Chicken (see p.130)
- Teriyaki Tofu (see p.84)
- Classic Egg-Fried Rice (see p.78)

Wash and pat dry the cucumber. Before cutting, bash the cucumber all over with the end of a rolling pin to crush the skin but not break it into pieces.

Trim the ends of the cucumber and slice it into bite-sized chunks or thick slices and place in a serving bowl.

Combine the cucumber with the soy sauce, black vinegar, sesame oil, garlic, sugar, salt and chilli oil. Allow to marinate for 5 minutes.

Scatter over the sesame seeds and spring onions and serve immediately as a side to Chinese five-spice chicken and/or teriyaki tofu with classic egg-fried rice.

BONUS

When you've dressed the cucumber in its marinade, avoid letting it sit for longer than 5 minutes. Otherwise liquid in the cucumber will be drawn out by the marinade and turn the dish watery.

# Shanghai Spring Onion Oil Noodles

●         ●
PREP:     COOK:
5 MINS    10 MINS

The humble spring onion (green onion) is the star and foundation of many Chinese dishes and, in particular, this Shanghai noodle recipe. My mum adores this noodle dish. She fed me bowls of it as a child, and to this day she still insists on ordering it whenever we stop by a classic Shanghai noodle joint on my trips back to China. It usually arrives almost immediately after placing an order because of how quick and easy it is to make - most of the work is in the preparation of the spring onions.

The fragrant and delicious sauce is a simple combo of storecupboard staples, but is packed with umami flavour. Oh, did I mention it is also vegan? For added protein, I sometimes top the noodles with Soy & Garlic Tofu Bites (see p.46) or for a meat-based alternative, shredded cooked chicken or turkey breast.

---

- 3 tbsp cooking oil of choice
- 3 spring onions (green onions), shredded
- 200g (7oz) dried wheat noodles (thin to medium-thick preferred)
- 2 tbsp light soy sauce
- ½ tbsp dark soy sauce
- 1 tsp granulated sugar
- salt, to taste

TO SERVE
-------------------------------

- ½ tsp toasted sesame seeds
- 1 tsp Easy Chilli Oil (see p.23), optional

PAIRING SUGGESTIONS
-------------------------------

- Soy & Garlic Tofu Bites (see p.46)
- Tomato & Egg Stir-Fry (see p.48)

Heat the cooking oil in a frying pan on a medium heat. Add the spring onions and fry gently for a few minutes until lightly browned. Remove the spring onions with chopsticks or tongs and set aside. Leave the oil in the pan to cool.

Meanwhile, cook the noodles in a pan of boiling water according to the packet instructions. Drain and rinse under cold running water, then set aside.

Add both types of soy sauce and the sugar to the cooled oil and stir to combine. Season to taste with salt, if needed.

Pour enough of the soy sauce mixture over the noodles to thoroughly coat them (you don't have to use all of it in one go), then toss until combined.

Scatter over the reserved fried spring onions with the sesame seeds and add a drizzle of chilli (chile) oil, if you like it spicy. Serve the noodles as a light meal or as part of a larger meal with soy and garlic tofu bites and a tomato and egg stir-fry.

# Creamy 10-Minute Peanut Noodles

**PREP:**
**5 MINS**

**COOK:**
**5 MINS**

Growing up in Shanghai, summers were hot and super humid and this really affected my appetite. When I wanted anything but warm food, my mum would hand me a bowl of cold noodles tossed in a luscious creamy sauce and topped with thinly sliced cucumber, which I'd slurp up in no time. I love this dish. It can easily be adapted to suit any taste, in particular a vegan diet, and is delicious with or without spice. It's also particularly good with white meat, like grilled chicken or turkey.

The creamy sauce is usually made with Chinese sesame paste, rice vinegar, light soy sauce and sugar, but since Chinese sesame paste isn't readily accessible, and tahini isn't quite the same, I often use peanut butter to get the same nutty flavour. I find the sauce delightfully addictive - it's something to do with the combination of savoury and the slight sweetness of the peanut butter.

I always have dried noodles, peanut butter and the other storecupboard ingredients to hand, so it's no surprise that this is one of my most go-to recipes.

---

- 200g (7oz) dried wheat noodles, such as Taiwanese knife-cut ribbon noodles

**FOR THE PEANUT SAUCE**
---------------------------------

- 2 tbsp light soy sauce
- 2 tbsp peanut butter
- ½ tbsp rice vinegar
- 1 tbsp sesame oil
- 1 garlic clove, minced

**TO SERVE**
---------------------------------

- 200g (7oz) steamed chicken breast, shredded, optional
- ½ tsp toasted sesame seeds
- 1 handful of chopped spring onions (green onions)
- 1 tsp Easy Chilli Oil (see p.23), optional

Cook the noodles in a pan of boiling water according to the packet instructions. Drain and rinse under cold running water, then set aside.

In a large mixing bowl, mix all the ingredients for the peanut sauce together, adding 1 tablespoon of water to loosen the mixture. If it's still too thick, add another 1 tablespoon of water.

Toss the cooked noodles in the peanut sauce, mixing thoroughly until evenly coated.

Spoon the peanut noodles into two serving bowls, top with the chicken, if using, and finish with the sesame seeds, spring onions and a splash of chilli (chile) oil, if you like. Serve straightaway.

# Soy & Garlic Tofu Bites

● ●
PREP:     COOK:
10 MINS*  15 MINS

*plus pressing tofu

Tofu has been a firm favourite of my family's since way back, and my Buddhist grandparents would always promote the idea of eating more veggies and beans over meat.

Tofu (soybean curd) is cooked in a myriad of ways in China, and other Asian countries too. It comes in different forms and textures, but for the first tofu recipe in this book, I want to introduce you to one of my favourite and tastiest ways to prepare it, and I'm proud to say that I've converted many tofu-haters with this recipe - it doesn't have to be bland and tasteless. The secret to great-tasting tofu is cornflour (cornstarch), which gives the tofu a crispy outer coating when fried, and makes a welcome contrast in texture as you bite into the soft inside.

---

- 350g (12oz) block of firm tofu, drained
- 25g (¼ cup) cornflour (cornstarch), more if needed
- 1 tsp sesame oil
- 2 tbsp light soy sauce
- 1 tsp rice vinegar
- 1 tsp granulated sugar
- 3 garlic cloves, minced
- 2 tbsp cooking oil of choice, plus extra if needed
- ½ tsp black sesame seeds
- ½ tbsp Easy Chilli Oil (see p.23), optional

### PAIRING SUGGESTIONS
----------------------------------

- Classic Egg-Fried Rice (see p.78)
- Sweet Soy Enoki Mushrooms (see p.86)

Drain the tofu well to remove any excess liquid, which would otherwise dilute the taste of the dish. If the tofu needs pressing, wrap it in a few sheets of kitchen paper and weigh it down with heavy plates. Leave it to drain for 30 minutes, then cut the tofu into bite-sized cubes.

Put the cornflour on a plate, add the tofu (in batches) and turn to generously coat the cubes on all sides. Pat off any excess cornflour.

In a bowl, mix together the sesame oil, soy sauce, rice vinegar, sugar and garlic, then set aside.

Heat the cooking oil in a large frying pan on a medium heat. Add the tofu and fry until light golden and crisp on all sides, about 10 minutes. Try not to move the tofu too much while frying, just turn it before it becomes too brown and make sure there are no uncooked patches of cornflour. Add more oil to the pan, if needed.

Pour the sauce over the tofu in the pan and gently turn until everything is combined.

Scatter the sesame seeds over the tofu and finish with a splash of chilli (chile) oil, if you like. Serve on its own or enjoy with classic egg-fried rice and sweet soy enoki mushrooms.

# Tomato & Egg Stir-Fry

● PREP: 5 MINS  ● COOK: 10 MINS

I don't know where I'd be without this dish. I'm pretty sure every single Chinese person has grown up eating it at least a few hundred times during their life.

While at university, I'd frequently turn to this dish, in the same way my flatmates would make beans on toast when they were hungry and strapped for cash. I'd argue that this tastes a lot better than beans on toast though, and it's cheap, easy and made with the simplest of ingredients!

The beauty of this recipe is the way the tangy tomatoes and fluffy scrambled eggs marry together in a combination of salt, sugar, sesame oil and oyster sauce - it's so addictive and moreish! Serve it on top of steamed rice.

---

- 2 tbsp cooking oil of choice
- 3 eggs, whisked
- 2 garlic cloves, finely chopped
- 2 beef tomatoes or 300g (10oz) regular tomatoes, chopped into wedges
- ¼ tsp salt
- 1 tsp granulated sugar
- pinch of MSG, optional
- ½ tsp sesame oil
- ½ tbsp oyster sauce
- 1 handful of chopped spring onions (green onions)
- Steamed Rice (see p.21), to serve

**PAIRING SUGGESTIONS**

- Soy & Garlic Tofu Bites (see p.46)
- Garlic Broccoli (see p.76)

Heat 1 tablespoon of the cooking oil in a large frying pan on a medium heat and add the eggs. Cook the eggs, stirring them gently until scrambled, breaking up any large pieces. Remove the eggs from the pan and set aside in a bowl.

In the same pan, heat the remaining oil, add the garlic and sauté, stirring, for 30 seconds, until fragrant. Add the tomatoes and cook for 2–3 minutes, until slightly softened.

Add the salt, sugar, MSG, if using, sesame oil and oyster sauce to the tomatoes and mix through. Cook until the tomatoes start to break down, adding a splash of water if it looks a bit dry.

Once the tomatoes are nice and saucy, return the eggs to the pan with the spring onions and cook, stirring until combined, for another 1–2 minutes, before serving with steamed rice. For a more substantial vegetarian meal, accompany with soy and garlic tofu bites and garlic broccoli.

# Yang-chun Mian

●  ●

PREP:  COOK:
5 MINS  5 MINS

Plain soup noodles, otherwise known as *yang-chun mian*,
is what my mum used to make for me all the time (you
can also use the term *yang-chun* to colloquially describe
someone as being plain and boring). So, if you think that
this dish could also be called "boring" noodles, you'd
be technically correct, but I prefer to say it makes
a great base for a noodle meal. I love adding dumplings
or wontons to my noodle soup, either frozen or homemade,
it doesn't matter.

The broth is a simple combination of salt, sugar, soy
sauce, sesame oil and spring onions (green onions) with
water, and is literally failproof, but if you want to
make it extra flavourful, swap out the water for some
good stock. I make poached chicken a lot, like my
Hainanese Chicken Rice (see p.160), so frequently use
the delicious leftover broth as a base for this soup.

---

- 200g (7oz) dried thin wheat
  noodles
- 1 tbsp light soy sauce
- 1 tsp dark soy sauce
- 1 tsp granulated sugar
- 2 tsp sesame oil
- 1 handful of chopped spring
  onions (green onions)
- 500ml (generous 2 cups)
  just-boiled water, or
  good-quality stock
- salt, to taste
- steamed leafy greens, such
  as pak choi (bok choy),
  to serve

PAIRING SUGGESTION
----------------------------------

- Pork & Prawn Wontons
  (see p.198)

Cook the noodles in a pan of boiling water according to the packet
instructions. Drain and rinse under cold running water, then set aside.

In a large heatproof bowl, combine both types of soy sauce with the
sugar, sesame oil and spring onions. Pour in the just-boiled water
or stock, stir and season with salt to taste.

Add the cooked noodles to the bowl and any toppings or extras you
like before serving. For a more substantial broth, add some pork
and prawn (shrimp) wontons (you may want to reduce the quantity
of noodles) as well as steamed leafy greens.

BONUS

Feel free to bulk out this
broth with some vegetables,
chicken or tofu - it's
basically a blank canvas
that can be customized to
whatever you like to eat.

# Dry Stir-Fried Green Beans

**PREP:**
**10 MINS**

**COOK:**
**12 MINS**

One of my favourite ways to eat green beans is this Sichuan-style dish. It is punchy in flavour thanks to the chilli (chile) and garlic, and it's pretty healthy too; the beans being dry stir-fried in a relatively small amount of oil compared to the traditional cooking method. If you order this in a Chinese restaurant, for instance, the green beans are typically deep-fried first, but I like to keep it simple and blister them in a hot wok or frying pan for a similar but lower-fat result.

Dry stir-frying also means no liquid, such as water, is added, so the flavour of the beans is not diluted and they retain a little bite, as well as a crispy texture from the slightly charred exterior.

---

- 3 tbsp cooking oil of choice, plus extra if needed
- 400g (14oz) green beans, trimmed
- 5 garlic cloves, minced
- 1 spring onion (green onion), finely chopped
- 1 bird's eye chilli (chile), or to taste
- ½ tsp salt
- ½ tsp granulated sugar
- pinch of MSG, optional

**PAIRING SUGGESTIONS**

--------------------------------

- Tomato & Egg Stir-Fry (see p.48)
- King Prawns in Ginger & Garlic (see p.61)

Heat the cooking oil in a large frying pan on a high heat until very hot. Add the green beans and cook for 4–5 minutes, until the beans blister on one side. Turn the beans over and cook for another 2–3 minutes . Try not to move the beans around too much during cooking, they should be slightly wrinkled and softened. Using a slotted spoon, remove the beans from the pan.

In the same pan, add a little more oil if it's a bit dry. Turn the heat down slightly, add the garlic, spring onion and chilli and cook until fragrant, about 1–2 minutes, taking care not to burn the garlic.

Toss the beans back in and add the salt, sugar and MSG, if using, and mix thoroughly. Check the seasoning and add more to taste, if needed, then serve as an accompaniment to the tomato and egg stir-fry and/or the king prawns (shrimp) in ginger and garlic.

# Chinese Hot Oil Noodles

●
**PREP:**
**5 MINS**

●
**COOK:**
**5 MINS**

You may have seen recipes for hot oil noodles, which literally translates as "oil splash noodles", on social media, but if you haven't, do add it to your roster of quick and easy meals.

The name comes from the method of pouring smoking hot oil over cooked noodles, garlic, chillies (chiles) and spring onions (green onions), so the flavourings instantly cook in the heat of the oil. The dish is then seasoned with soy sauce and Chinese black vinegar, and it's honestly as simple as that. As with many recipes in this book, the noodles can easily be adapted to suit your dietary preferences, and for a more substantial meal, add protein, such as cooked chicken or fried tofu.

- 150g (5½oz) dried wheat noodles (I like knife-cut noodles for their pretty shape, see p.17)
- 2 spring onions (green onions), finely chopped
- 3 garlic cloves, minced
- 1 tsp dried Sichuan chilli flakes (see p.12)
- ¼ tsp salt
- 2 tbsp cooking oil of choice
- 1 tbsp light soy sauce
- 1 tsp Chinese black vinegar
- steamed pak choi (bok choy) or other leafy greens, to serve

## PAIRING SUGGESTIONS
----------------------------------

- Chinese Five-Spice Chicken (see p.130)
- Smacked Cucumber (see p.40)

Cook the noodles in a pan of boiling water according to the packet instructions. Drain and rinse under cold running water and place in a large serving bowl.

Place the spring onions, garlic, chilli and salt in a pile on top of the cooked noodles.

Heat the oil in a frying pan until smoking hot. Remove the pan from the heat and carefully pour the oil directly over the top of the seasonings in the bowl of noodles.

Add the soy sauce and black vinegar and toss everything together thoroughly, making sure the noodles are evenly coated. Serve with Chinese five-spice chicken and smacked cucumber, if you like.

# Lettuce in Oyster & Garlic Sauce

**PREP:**
5 MINS

**COOK:**
10 MINS

One of the best ways to cook lettuce is in oyster sauce. It's a great way to enjoy a big serving of veg, and the sweet flavour and crisp texture of the romaine or iceberg lettuce really comes through. Feel free to switch the lettuce for pak choi (bok choy), if you prefer - it works really nicely thanks to the combination of leafy green and crisp stalk. Vegans and vegetarians could also swap the oyster sauce for mushroom stir-fry sauce, which has a similar flavour profile.

- 1-2 heads romaine or iceberg lettuce, or pak choi (bok choy)
- 2 tbsp cooking oil of choice
- 3 garlic cloves, minced
- 1 tbsp oyster sauce or mushroom stir-fry sauce
- ½ tbsp light soy sauce
- ½ tsp granulated sugar
- ¼ tsp salt
- Steamed Rice (see p.21), to serve

### PAIRING SUGGESTIONS
--------------------------------

- Soy & Garlic Tofu Bites (see p.46)
- Crispy Sea Bass (see p.142)

Wash and separate the lettuce leaves or pak choi, keeping the latter whole.

Bring a saucepan of water to the boil. Add the lettuce leaves to the pan and blanch for no longer than 30 seconds, until just wilted (pak choi may take slightly longer, about 1 minute). Remove the leaves from the hot water and briefly refresh under cold running water for a few seconds. Shake off any excess and place on a serving plate.

In a small frying pan, heat the cooking oil on a medium heat and gently sauté the garlic until fragrant.

Add the oyster sauce or mushroom stir-fry sauce, soy sauce, sugar and salt. Pour in 1 tablespoon of water and stir until combined. Once the sauce has warmed through and slightly thickened, remove from the heat.

To serve, pour the sauce over the blanched lettuce leaves or pak choi and enjoy alongside some steamed rice with the soy and garlic tofu bites and crispy sea bass, if liked.

# Yaki Udon

● PREP: 10 MINS     ● COOK: 20 MINS

This tasty, popular Japanese noodle dish is made with thick and chewy udon noodles. It's one of my go-to dishes for making ahead, and sometimes I even prepare a big batch to freeze in portions. Knowing that I have a complete meal ready prepared always makes me excited for lunch, whether it's in the office, or a more relaxed working from home.

The chunky noodles are stir-fried in a sweet and umami-rich sauce and in this recipe I've added tender, juicy slices of chicken thigh.

---

- 400g (14oz) fresh udon noodles, preferably vacuum-packed
- 3 tbsp cooking oil of choice
- 1 small brown onion, thinly sliced
- 3-4 garlic cloves, minced
- 2cm (¾in) piece of fresh root ginger, peeled and thinly sliced
- 250g (9oz) skinless boneless chicken thighs, thinly sliced
- 1 carrot, cut into julienne strips
- 3-4 shiitake mushrooms, thinly sliced
- 3-4 white cabbage leaves, thinly sliced
- 1 large handful of chopped spring onions (green onions)
- 1 tsp toasted sesame seeds or shichimi togarashi, to finish

FOR THE STIR-FRY SAUCE
---------------------------------

- 5 tbsp light soy sauce
- ½ tbsp dark soy sauce
- 2 tbsp mirin
- ½ tsp sesame oil

Mix all the ingredients for the sauce together and set aside.

Soak the udon noodles in a bowl of hot water for 5 minutes, separating them if needed. (There is no need to cook the udon at this point as it may cause them to overcook when stir-fried.) Drain and set aside.

Meanwhile, heat 2 tablespoons of the cooking oil in a large frying pan or wok on a medium–high heat. Add the onion and sauté until translucent. Add the garlic and ginger and sauté for a few minutes longer until aromatic.

In the same pan or wok, make some space in the centre, pushing the contents to the edges, then add the remaining cooking oil. Add the chicken and stir-fry for 5–7 minutes, until it is no longer pink in appearance.

Toss in the carrot, shiitake mushrooms and cabbage and stir-fry for 3–4 minutes, until softened.

Add the cooked noodles and sauce. Mix everything thoroughly, add a splash of water if it's a little dry, then heat through.

When just about ready, throw in the spring onions and turn off the heat. Sprinkle over the sesame seeds or shichimi togarashi and serve immediately.

# King Prawns in Ginger & Garlic

Although my parents argued a lot about various things while I was growing up, they both agreed that I needed to eat more seafood; "because it makes you clever", they would nod in agreement. I've always been a fan of the meaty texture and flavour of prawns (shrimp), so I'd happily eat them in various dishes. This one can be made in a flash, and uses staple Chinese ingredients, yet still manages to retain the fresh, natural sweetness of the prawns. It makes enough for two people, but I could easily eat it all - my parents would approve, for sure.

**PREP:**
10 MINS

**COOK:**
10 MINS

- 1 tbsp cooking oil of choice
- 2cm (¾in) piece of fresh root ginger, peeled and finely chopped
- 5 garlic cloves, finely chopped
- 20 peeled raw king prawns (shrimp), deveined
- 1 handful of chopped spring onions (green onions)
- 1 tbsp light soy sauce
- 1 tbsp Chinese cooking wine

**TO SERVE**
- - - - - - - - - - - - - - - - - - - - - - - -
- Steamed Rice (see p.21)
- steamed pak choi (bok choy)
- Easy Chilli Oil (see p.23)

**PAIRING SUGGESTIONS**
- - - - - - - - - - - - - - - - - - - - - - - -
- Garlic Broccoli (see p.76)
- Tomato & Egg Stir-Fry (see p.48)

Heat the oil in a large frying pan on a medium heat. Add the ginger and garlic and sauté for about 30 seconds, stirring occasionally to prevent the garlic burning.

Add the prawns and sauté for 4–5 minutes, turning once, until they turn pink and are cooked through.

Add the spring onions, soy sauce and cooking wine, then stir to combine.

Serve piping hot and enjoy with steamed rice and a side of green vegetables, such as steamed pak choi or garlic broccoli, and a spoonful of chilli oil. For a more substantial meal, accompany with a tomato and egg stir-fry.

# Chinese Scrambled Eggs with Prawn

**PREP:**
5 MINS*

**COOK:**
5 MINS

*plus marinating

My time at university was often spent budgeting for groceries and trying to eat something other than baked beans on toast. It will come as no surprise then to discover that my meals often featured this dish, which I've loved eating since childhood.

My mum makes the best scrambled eggs - super silky and soft. The secret ingredient, as told by my mother, is the cornflour (cornstarch) water, which tenderizes the egg and keeps the protein strands separate. This stops the eggs becoming rubbery during the cooking process, she tells me convincingly with her background in chemistry. The result is a fantastically soft and satisfying scrambled egg, and a great time-saving meal.

---

- 6-8 peeled raw king prawns (shrimp), deveined
- 1 tsp Chinese cooking wine
- pinch of salt and freshly ground black pepper
- 1 tbsp cornflour (cornstarch)
- 3 eggs
- 3 tbsp cooking oil of choice

**TO SERVE**

- 1 handful of shredded spring onions (green onions)
- ½ tsp toasted sesame seeds
- 1 tsp Easy Chilli Oil (see p.23), optional
- Steamed Rice (see p.21), optional

**PAIRING SUGGESTIONS**

- Sweet Soy Enoki Mushrooms (see p.86)
- Fish-Fragrant Aubergine (see p.88)

Put the prawns in a shallow dish, pour over the Chinese cooking wine and season with a pinch of salt and pepper. Mix to combine and leave to marinate for around 10 minutes.

Mix the cornflour with 2 tablespoons of water in a small bowl, then beat into the eggs until well combined.

Heat 1 tablespoon of the oil in a large frying pan or wok on a medium heat. Add the prawns and cook, turning once, for 2 minutes, until pink. Add the prawns to the egg mixture.

Heat the remaining oil in the frying pan or wok until steaming hot. Pour in the egg and prawn mixture and immediately turn the heat down to low. Gently push the egg from the outer edges towards the centre with a spatula, so it gathers slightly in the middle. Cook, stirring gently, for around 2–3 minutes in total, until the egg scrambles but is still slightly runny in parts. Remove the pan from the heat.

Sprinkle over the spring onions and sesame seeds, then add a splash of chilli oil, if using. Serve over rice or eat plain. For an excellent vegetarian spread, serve with sweet soy enoki mushrooms and fish-fragrant aubergine (eggplant).

# Easy Braised Pork Ribs

● PREP:
5 MINS

● COOK:
45 MINS

Every student has something that got them through uni or student life, be it budget alcohol, cheap pot noodles, beans on toast, or an amalgamation of the above. For me, it was braised pork ribs. I have made this time and time again and it's also a dish I've passed on to countless friends and flatmates because it's so easy and can be meal-prepped in advance. The combination of simple everyday ingredients, such as sugar, garlic and soy sauce, with the pork make this one of the most foolproof recipes. It's also a dish that gets better with time - like so many things in life. Just make sure you buy good-quality pork ribs, by that I mean ones with a generous ratio of meat-to-bone.

If you're not a fan of pork, this would also work well with other proteins, such as chicken wings, and can easily be adapted to suit non-meat eaters, be it with tofu or other plant-based alternatives.

---

- 2 tbsp cooking oil of choice
- 750g-1kg (1lb 10oz-2¼lb) pork ribs
- 4 garlic cloves, roughly chopped
- 4 tbsp light soy sauce
- 1 tbsp granulated sugar
- 1 handful of chopped spring onions (green onions)
- salt, to taste
- pinch of MSG, optional

TO SERVE
---------------------------------
- steamed choi sum, optional
- toasted sesame seeds
- Steamed Rice (see p.21)

PAIRING SUGGESTIONS
---------------------------------
- Lettuce in Oyster & Garlic Sauce (see p.56)
- Sweet Soy Enoki Mushrooms (see p.86)

Heat the cooking oil on a medium heat in a large wok or saucepan. Add half the ribs and sear for about 2–3 minutes, until lightly browned all over. Remove and repeat with the rest of the ribs, adding more oil, if needed.

Once the ribs are lightly browned, add the garlic, soy sauce and sugar to the pan and mix thoroughly until combined.

Pour in 750ml (3 cups) of water and turn the heat to low. Simmer the ribs for about 30 minutes, stirring every now and then to ensure they are evenly submerged as they cook. Top up with extra water, when needed.

After 30 minutes, turn the heat up so the liquid comes to the boil and cook until reduced and thickened, leaving some to spoon over as a sauce when ready to serve. This should take no more than 5 minutes. Throw in the spring onions and season with salt and MSG, if using.

Serve the ribs with choi sum sprinkled with sesame seeds, if you like, and steamed rice. Spoon over any sauce from the pan. For a larger meal, swap the choi sum for lettuce in oyster and garlic sauce and serve with sweet soy enoki mushrooms on the side.

# Set Menu

.

→ TOMATO & EGG STIR-FRY (48)

→ DRY STIR-FRIED GREEN BEANS (53)

→ CHINESE HOT OIL NOODLES (54)

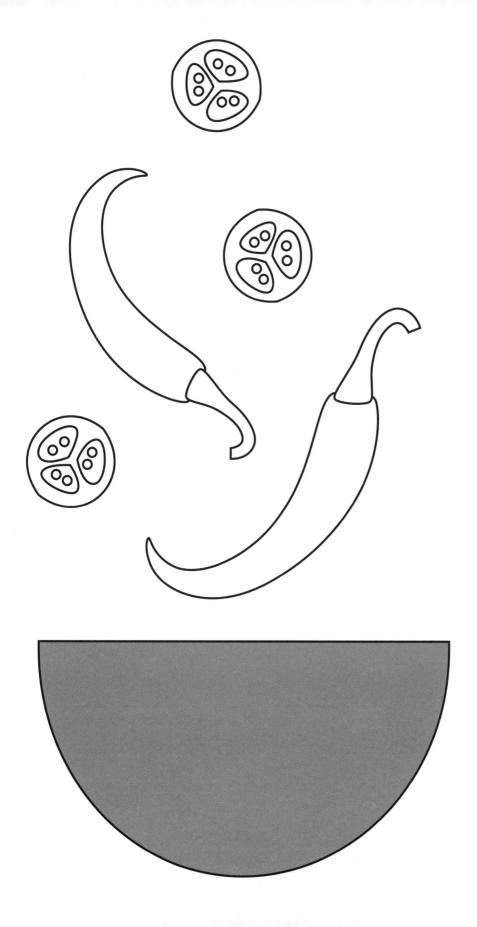

# Finding

# Balance

# Finding Balance

Given my family's strong belief in Buddhism, which advocates the avoidance of suffering and non-violence, vegetarian dishes were plentiful at every meal to add balance to any meat or fish dishes.

After my parents officially separated and the court gave Dad custody of me, my mum stayed in Shanghai. Aged seven, I moved to Hangzhou, a city near Shanghai, where my dad and his side of the family is from. This was so that I could live with my aunt, uncle, cousin and grandparents for a few years while he set up home in the UK for the first time. For that period, my aunt and uncle adopted me as their own, so for two years I had a complete family unit, and it felt nice to not have to listen to arguing all the time. My dad's side of the family were mostly Buddhists, which meant that there were mini pagodas and statues of Guan Yin, the goddess of compassion, mercy and kindness in their homes.

My grandma was a good cook, but strangely enough my aunt wasn't – my uncle, however, was the real star in the kitchen. I used to think how peculiar it was to see a man in the kitchen rustling up tons of delicious food, especially since my own father didn't know how to cook. But now looking back, I think he was such a gem. Each dinner time I'd feel excited to see what he'd cooked up that day. The kitchen was small in their apartment so the smell of cooking would pleasantly waft through every room. On weekends, I'd join him and my aunt at the fresh markets to see which ingredients they'd pick, just so I'd get a hint of what was going to be on the dinner menu that night.

It was a similar scene at my grandma's house, where I stayed occasionally. She and Grandad would help each other in the kitchen, occasionally bickering about something trivial like where he had misplaced the soup spoon. In the winter, the whole place would become steamy as pots of braised pork alongside winter melon soup simmered away, warming up the room.

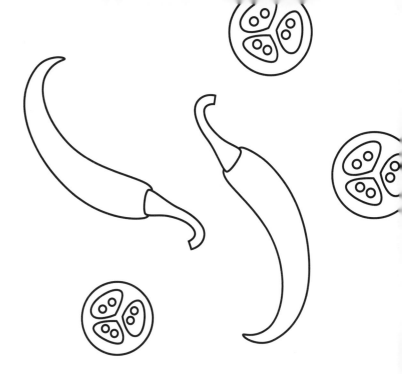

On occasion, my aunt, uncle and cousin would come to my grandparents' place to join us for dinner. There'd be six of us crowded around a table, pulling in an extra chair or two so that we'd all fit. My cousin and I both loved a classic Red Braised Pork Belly (see p.110), so much that we would often fight over the best piece, especially if it had a chunky layer of pork fat attached. Whenever this happened, my grandad would try to find another piece that looked just as good so we'd both be happy.

Given my family's strong belief in Buddhism, which advocates the avoidance of suffering and non-violence, vegetarian dishes were plentiful at every meal to add balance to any meat or fish dishes. Tofu, too, was a frequently used ingredient in many different dishes, and was presented in various shapes, flavours and textures. Silken tofu was my favourite growing up because it's delicious both hot or cold; it jiggles like a panna cotta when you first turn it out from the box and the texture is so smooth and delicate it literally melts in your mouth. Silken tofu makes a great addition to soups and broths as it doesn't need any preparation, other than cutting it into cubes – just slurp it up like you would noodles.

If you're reading this and thinking how unappetizing tofu is, let me help change your mind. I've got a few great recipes up my sleeve like Teriyaki Tofu (see p.84), made with firm tofu, which is readily available in blocks in supermarkets, health food shops and Asian food stores. Or there's a very refreshing recipe for Cold Silken Tofu (see p.74), which makes a great side dish to any Asian meal, especially on a hot and humid day. Both of these recipes can be found in this chapter, and I hope will encourage you to love tofu as much as me.

# Cold Silken Tofu

 凉拌豆腐

●
**PREP:**
**10 MINS**

I love tofu. In my eyes, it's super versatile and a great addition to all meals. The idea of eating it cold may be a little strange to some, but silken tofu is one of my favourite types as it is so delicate and soft in texture; a bit like a savoury panna cotta.

This recipe requires no cooking and only calls for a few staple ingredients. The spicy and tangy sauce in contrast to the cold, mild-tasting tofu makes this dish especially great for hot summer weather.

- 2 tbsp Ginger & Spring Onion Sauce (see p.25)
- 1 bird's eye chilli (chile), deseeded and chopped
- 1 tbsp light soy sauce
- 1 tbsp (vegan) oyster sauce or mushroom stir-fry sauce
- ½ tbsp Chinese black vinegar, or rice vinegar
- 300g (10oz) silken tofu, drained

**TO SERVE**
- - - - - - - - - - - - - - - - - - - - - - - - - - - - - - -
- 1 tsp toasted sesame seeds
- 1 handful of coriander (cilantro) leaves and/or chopped spring onions (green onions)

**PAIRING SUGGESTIONS**
- - - - - - - - - - - - - - - - - - - - - - - - - - - - - - -
- Classic Egg-Fried Rice (see p.78)
- Chinese Five-Spice Chicken (see p.130)

In a small bowl, combine the ginger and spring onion sauce with the chilli, soy sauce, oyster sauce or mushroom stir-fry sauce and vinegar, then mix until combined.

Place the silken tofu on a serving plate and leave whole or carefully slice a few times to cut into cubes. Pour the chilli sauce over the tofu, making sure some goes down the sides.

Finish with a scattering of toasted sesame seeds and coriander and/or spring onions. Serve with classic egg-fried rice and/or Chinese five-spice chicken.

SERVES 2

# Garlic Broccoli

## PREP: 5 MINS  COOK: 10 MINS

Broccoli is my favourite vegetable (when I'm in the UK) and this dish is typically the first thing I eat when I get back from any kind of overseas trip. For some reason, I really crave it whenever I'm away, and tucking into a bowl of steamed rice, a crispy-edged fried egg and garlicky broccoli feels likes a super-nourishing and delicious welcome home.

It's the perfect side dish to almost everything in this book, but take care not to overcook the broccoli when blanching as it won't be so tasty.

- 1 head of broccoli, a 250g (9oz), cut into florets
- 2 tbsp cooking oil of choice
- 3 garlic cloves, finely chopped
- ½ tbsp dried shrimp, optional
- 1 small carrot, thinly sliced diagonally
- pinch of MSG, optional
- salt, to taste

PAIRING SUGGESTION
---------------------------------
- can be served with most dishes in this book

Place the broccoli florets in a pan filled with cold water and bring to the boil. Once the water is boiling, drain immediately and rinse the broccoli briefly under cold running water. Set aside.

Heat the cooking oil in a large frying pan on a medium heat. Add the garlic and dried shrimp and sauté for a minute or two until fragrant.

Add the carrot and continue to stir-fry for a few minutes before adding the blanched broccoli. Cook for another 2 minutes, until the veg is just tender.

Season with salt, to taste, and serve immediately as a side to almost any recipe in this book.

BONUS

Pak choi (bok choy) would also be fab here instead of broccoli. Just wash and roughly chop the leaves and stalk into bite-sized pieces and skip the blanching step.

# Classic Egg-Fried Rice

**PREP:**
5 MINS

**COOK:**
15 MINS

This dish needs little in the way of introduction…
a simple, yet delicious, meal of egg-fried rice hits
the spot every time. It's quick to whip up and a great
way to use up leftovers in the fridge, making it super
adaptable to suit all dietary preferences.

Feel free to switch the vegetables used here or
throw in some cubes of tofu, cooked strips of chicken
or crispy pieces of bacon for extra flavour and protein.

---

- 3 tbsp cooking oil of
  choice
- 3 large eggs, whisked
- 1 small carrot, finely diced
- 50g (⅓ cup) garden peas,
  fresh or frozen
- 350g (1¾ cups) cold cooked
  Thai or Japanese rice, or
  your rice of choice
- ½ tbsp light soy sauce
- ½ tsp sesame oil
- ¼ tsp ground white pepper
- pinch of MSG, optional
- 2 spring onions (green
  onions), finely chopped
- salt, to taste

### PAIRING SUGGESTIONS
----------------------------------

- Teriyaki Tofu (see p.84)
- Honey Garlic Chicken
  (see p.118)

Heat 2 tablespoons of the cooking oil in a large frying pan or wok
on a medium heat. Add the whisked eggs and cook, stirring gently,
until lightly scrambled. Roughly break up the egg into smaller
pieces, spoon into a bowl and set aside.

In the same pan or wok, heat the remaining cooking oil and stir-fry
the carrot for 3–4 minutes, until slightly softened, followed by the
peas for another minute.

Stir in the cold cooked rice and heat thoroughly for 4–5 minutes,
breaking up any clumps of rice with a spatula, until piping hot.

Add the scrambled eggs with the soy sauce, sesame oil, white
pepper and MSG, if using, then mix thoroughly until combined.
Throw in the spring onions and stir through one last time.

Taste and add salt, if needed, and serve as a side to teriyaki
tofu and honey garlic chicken.

# Chilli & Lime Salmon Rice Bowl

**PREP:**
**15 MINS**

**COOK:**
**20 MINS**

Salmon is my go-to when it comes to fish. It's perfect for when I'm short on time, but want something healthy and filling. I like to cook salmon in a teriyaki sauce (see my Teriyaki Tofu on p.84) or maybe in honey and garlic (similar to my Honey Garlic Chicken on p.118), but here it's marinated, which doubles up as a light dressing. The chilli (chile), lime, honey and fish sauce marinade is inspired by Vietnamese and Thai cuisines, and I really like the freshness it brings, while not missing out on the umami flavour. Served over rice with an egg, pickled veg and avocado, this salmon bowl feels like one you would get in a restaurant.

---

- 2 salmon fillets
- ½ tsp salt
- 200g (generous 1 cup) Japanese short-grain rice
- 1 tbsp cooking oil of choice

## FOR THE MARINADE
-------------------------------------

- 1 mild red chilli (chile), deseeded and finely chopped
- 1 garlic clove, minced
- juice and finely grated zest of 1 lime
- 1 tbsp fish sauce
- 1 tbsp honey or maple syrup

## TO SERVE
-------------------------------------

- 30g (1oz) Pickled Cucumber and/or Pickled Carrot & Daikon (see pp.27 and 28)
- ½ ripe avocado, peeled, stone removed and cubed
- 2 Japanese Soy-Marinated Eggs (see p.31), halved
- 1 sheet toasted nori seaweed, shredded
- ½ tsp toasted sesame seeds
- salt, to taste
- coriander (cilantro) leaves

Mix the ingredients for the marinade together in a bowl, take out 2 tablespoons and set aside for later – this will be used to make the dressing.

Pat dry the salmon fillets, place on a plate and season with the salt. Pour the marinade over the fish, give it a good rub and set aside to marinate for 10 minutes. Flip the salmon over halfway through to ensure both sides are coated.

While the salmon is marinating, cook the Japanese rice according to the packet instructions, or follow the method for Steamed Rice (see p.21).

Heat the cooking oil in a frying pan on a medium-high heat. When hot, fry the salmon, skin-side down, for 3–4 minutes. Leave the fish to sear undisturbed until the skin becomes crispy, then flip it over to cook for another 3–4 minutes, or until cooked to your liking. Add any marinade left on the plate and spoon it over and around the salmon, then heat through briefly.

Meanwhile, to assemble the dish, spoon the rice into two serving bowls. Divide the pickled vegetables, avocado and soy-marinated eggs between the bowls, placing them on top of the rice.

To serve, place the salmon in the serving bowls and sprinkle over the nori seaweed and sesame seeds, then spoon over the reserved marinade to make a dressing. Finish with a few coriander leaves.

# Seared Sweetheart Cabbage

**PREP:**
**10 MINS**

**COOK:**
**10 MINS**

Cabbage is so underrated, versatile and delicious. Sweetheart (or hispi) cabbage joins broccoli and pak choi (bok choy) as my favourite vegetables in the UK.

I first made this simple cabbage dish during Veganuary, 2021, and it was something I threw together on a grey afternoon during a quick lunchtime cooking session between meetings. When I took my first mouthful, I instantly knew it was a winner!

---

- 2 tbsp cooking oil of choice
- 1 sweetheart cabbage, quartered lengthways
- 3 garlic cloves, finely chopped
- 1 mild red chilli (chile), deseeded and finely chopped
- 1 spring onion (green onion), finely chopped
- 1 tbsp sesame oil
- 2 tbsp light soy sauce
- 1 tbsp (vegan) oyster sauce or mushroom stir-fry sauce
- ⅛ tsp granulated sugar
- salt, to taste
- Steamed Rice (see p.21), to serve (optional)

### PAIRING SUGGESTIONS
----------------------------------

- Black Pepper Tofu
  (see p.90)
- Fish-Fragrant Aubergine
  (see p88)
- Kimchi Fried Rice
  (see p.116)

Heat 1 tablespoon of the cooking oil in a large frying pan (with a lid) on a medium–high heat until hot. Place the cabbage, flat-side down, in the pan and sear for 1–2 minutes, until lightly browned. Turn the cabbage over and cook it on the other flat side for the same length of time.

Turn the heat to medium and add 3 tablespoons of water to the pan. Cover with a lid and steam-cook the cabbage for 4–5 minutes, until tender. Remove the cabbage and place on a serving plate.

While the cabbage is cooking, heat the remaining cooking oil in a small saucepan on a medium-low heat. Add the garlic, chilli and spring onion and stir-fry until fragrant. Add the sesame oil, soy sauce, oyster sauce or mushroom stir-fry sauce and sugar. Stir until the sugar dissolves, then remove from the heat. Taste and adjust with salt, if needed.

Pour the sauce all over the seared cabbage and serve as part of a larger meal with black pepper tofu, fish-fragrant aubergine (eggplant) and kimchi fried rice or plain steamed rice.

**BONUS**

Instead of searing the quartered cabbage, shred it and stir-fry in the same seasonings. This will make the cabbage easier to portion if you're meal prepping for the week ahead.

# Teriyaki Tofu

照烧豆腐

**PREP:**
**15 MINS***

**COOK:**
**15 MINS**

*plus pressing tofu

Inspired by the Japanese snack - the norimaki senbei rice cracker - this is my most popular recipe on Instagram by far, and with good reason. The teriyaki tofu is wrapped in a strip of nori for the ultimate umami flavour bomb and contrast in texture. If you've never liked tofu, try this and let me change your mind!

---

- 300g (10oz) block of firm tofu, drained
- 1-2 sheets nori seaweed, cut into strips for wrapping around tofu
- 4 tbsp cornflour (cornstarch), plus extra if needed
- 3-4 tbsp cooking oil of choice

**FOR THE TERIYAKI SAUCE**

- 1 tbsp mirin
- 1 tbsp light soft brown sugar or runny honey
- 3 tbsp light soy sauce

**TO SERVE**

- ½ tsp toasted sesame seeds
- Steamed Rice (see p.21), optional

**PAIRING SUGGESTIONS**

- Dry Stir-Fried Green Beans (see p.53)
- King Prawns in Ginger & Garlic (see p.61)

To remove any excess water in the tofu, wrap it in a few sheets of kitchen paper, place in a shallow dish and weigh down with heavy plates. Leave to drain for 30 minutes.

While the tofu is draining, combine the ingredients for the teriyaki sauce with 3 tablespoons of water in a bowl and set aside.

Slice the drained tofu into chunky equal-sized sticks, about 12–15 in total. Cut the nori sheets into narrow rectangular strips, long enough to wrap around the tofu sticks.

Fill a shallow dish with water and lightly dip a piece of nori in the water until damp, but not too wet. Take the dampened strip of nori and wrap it around the middle of the tofu – the water will make the nori pliable and help it to stick more readily – leaving the ends of the tofu exposed. Repeat until all the tofu sticks are wrapped in nori. Set aside.

Tip the cornflour into a clean shallow bowl. Dunk each piece of wrapped tofu into the cornflour to generously cover all sides, then pat off any excess.

Heat 2 tablespoons of the cooking oil in a large frying pan on a medium heat. Gently fry the tofu, turning occasionally and adding more cooking oil when needed, until golden brown on all sides, and there are no uncooked patches of cornflour. This takes around 10 minutes in total.

When all the tofu is evenly browned, turn the heat to low and pour over the teriyaki sauce. Allow the sauce to sizzle and thicken, turning the tofu to ensure all sides are evenly coated.

Sprinkle the sesame seeds over and serve immediately as a tasty snack. For a more substantial meal, serve the tofu with steamed rice, dry stir-fried green beans and king prawns (shrimp) in ginger and garlic.

# Sweet Soy Enoki Mushrooms

**PREP:**
5 MINS

**COOK:**
5 MINS

It's likely that both you and I have a mushroom-hating friend; "it's the texture," they say. Well, one time I made this dish for my anti-mushroom friend without telling her she was eating enoki mushrooms and she said it was delicious - I felt very proud of myself.

Long, thin, mild-tasting enoki mushrooms come in bundles and have long been popular in Asian cooking, including Japan, China and South Korea. They are also commonly used in hot-pot restaurants where the enoki are blanched briefly in broth and readily take on the flavours of the ingredients that they are cooked with.

You can typically find them fresh and vacuum-packed in Asian supermarkets and some large supermarkets. Prior to cooking, simply trim the roots and give the mushrooms a quick rinse in a bowl of water to remove any earth.

---

- 200g (7oz) enoki mushrooms
- 1 tbsp cooking oil of choice
- 2 garlic cloves, minced
- 1 spring onion (green onion), finely chopped, white and green parts separated
- 1 tbsp light soy sauce
- 1 tsp (vegan) oyster sauce or mushroom stir-fry sauce
- 1 tsp granulated sugar
- salt, to taste
- Steamed Rice (see p.21), to serve

### PAIRING SUGGESTIONS

- Black Pepper Tofu (see p.90)
- Sichuan Dry Pot Potatoes (see p.112)
- Crispy Chicken & Leek Noodles (see p.124)

Trim about 2.5cm (1in) off the root end of the enoki mushrooms and discard. Wash carefully and separate the mushrooms into slightly smaller bundles.

Bring a frying pan half-filled with water to the boil and blanch the enoki mushrooms for 1 minute. Remove with a slotted spoon and drain, gently squeezing out any water, then place on a serving plate.

Heat the cooking oil in a small pan on a medium heat. Add the garlic and white part of the spring onion and stir-fry for 30 seconds, until fragrant. Pour in the soy sauce, oyster sauce or mushroom stir-fry sauce and sugar with ½ tablespoon of water. Stir to combine. Once the sugar dissolves, which only takes about 30 seconds, toss in the green part of the spring onion and give everything one last stir.

Adjust the seasoning to taste, adding salt if needed. Remove the pan from the heat and carefully pour the sauce over the blanched enoki mushrooms.

Serve with steamed rice and other dishes, such as black pepper tofu, Sichuan dry pot potatoes and crispy chicken and leek noodles for a feast.

SERVES 2

# Fish-Fragrant Aubergine

鱼香茄子

Before you say anything, there is no trace of fish in this dish. The reason for its quirky name is down to a really interesting tale, and the story goes like this… In the city of Dazhou, Sichuan Province, there was a family who loved to eat fish. They were very particular about how their fish was cooked and regularly used ingredients such as ginger, spring onions (green onions), garlic, vinegar, soy sauce and cooking wine. One night, the wife had nothing to cook but leftovers, and so served these up disguised with leftover fish seasonings. Her husband found the dish delicious and eventually she confessed that the meal wasn't fish at all, but "fish-fragrant". Subsequently, over the years, the dish has been altered and adapted to become a classic in Sichuan cuisine.

If you order this at a Chinese restaurant, you may find a myriad of options, such as fish-fragrant pork, fish-fragrant liver or fish-fragrant aubergine (eggplant). I personally love it with aubergine, since when braised it becomes silky and tender as it absorbs the luscious spicy sauce. The aubergine is so good it's borderline addictive - you've got to try it!

---

- 1 large aubergine (eggplant), cut into 7.5cm (3in) long wedges
- ½ tsp salt
- 4 tbsp cooking oil of choice
- 3 garlic cloves, finely chopped
- 1 tbsp finely chopped fresh root ginger
- 1 small red chilli (chile), roughly chopped
- 1 handful of chopped spring onions (green onions)
- Steamed Rice (see p.21), to serve

FOR THE BRAISING SAUCE
- - - - - - - - - - - - - - - - - - - - - - - -

- 1 tbsp Chinese black vinegar
- 1 tbsp light soy sauce
- 1 tbsp granulated sugar
- ½ tbsp Chinese spicy bean paste (doubanjiang), or add 1 tbsp light soy sauce

PAIRING SUGGESTIONS
- - - - - - - - - - - - - - - - - - - - - - - -

- Seared Sweetheart Cabbage (see p.82)
- Chinese Five-Spice Chicken (see p.130)

Place the aubergine in a large bowl and sprinkle over the salt. Leave the aubergine for around 10 minutes to draw out any water and prevent bitterness.

Meanwhile, mix the ingredients for the braising sauce with 3 tablespoons of water in a bowl and set aside.

By now the aubergine should have released some of its moisture, so pat it dry with kitchen paper.

Heat 2 tablespoons of the cooking oil in a large frying pan or wok (with a lid) on a medium–high heat. Add the aubergine and stir-fry for 6–7 minutes, until lightly browned all over. Remove from the pan and set aside.

In the same pan or wok, heat the remaining oil and sauté the garlic, ginger and chilli until fragrant.

Return the aubergine to the pan or wok, followed by the braising sauce and turn the heat down. Cover with a lid and simmer for 5-10 minutes, until the aubergine is nice and soft.

Throw in the spring onions and stir to combine, and it's now ready to serve with steamed rice. For a more substantial meal, serve with seared sweetheart cabbage and Chinese five-spice chicken.

# Black Pepper Tofu

● ●
PREP:    COOK:
10 MINS* 15 MINS

*plus pressing the tofu

Black pepper beef is a classic Chinese stir-fry dish. The simple combination of freshly ground black pepper with soy sauce and oyster sauce makes it an incredibly tasty way to cook beef. Here, I've adapted the recipe to make it vegan, using firm tofu instead. The chunky pieces of tofu are dusted in cornflour (cornstarch) and pan-fried until crisp, so it takes on a great texture and all the flavours of the sauce.

You can totally make this in the traditional way with beef slices, if preferred, but trust me, it's also totally delicious plant-based, and it may just convert those who don't like tofu!

---

- 350g (12oz) block of firm tofu, drained
- 2 tbsp light soy sauce
- 1 tbsp (vegan) oyster sauce or mushroom stir-fry sauce
- 3 garlic cloves, minced
- 2cm (¾in) piece of fresh root ginger, finely chopped
- 1-2 tbsp freshly ground black pepper
- 5 tbsp cornflour (cornstarch)
- 2 tbsp cooking oil of choice
- 1 small handful of finely chopped spring onions (green onions)
- Steamed Rice (see p.21), to serve

PAIRING SUGGESTIONS
---------------------------------
- Seared Sweetheart Cabbage (see p.82)
- Miso Aubergine (see p.97)

To remove any excess water in the tofu, wrap it in a few sheets of kitchen paper, place in a shallow dish and weigh down with heavy plates. Leave to drain for 30 minutes.

While the tofu is draining, mix the soy sauce and oyster sauce with the garlic, ginger, black pepper and 3 tablespoons of water. Set aside until later.

Cut the drained tofu into pieces, about 2cm (¾in) thick.

Tip the cornflour into a shallow dish. Dunk each piece of tofu into the cornflour to generously coat all sides, then pat off any excess.

Heat the oil in a large frying pan on a medium–high heat until hot. Add the tofu and fry for 4–5 minutes on each side, until golden brown and crisp, and there are no visible patches of cornflour.

Turn the heat down to low and pour in the sauce. Let it simmer away until the sauce has reduced and thickened, then flip the tofu over so both sides are coated in the sauce.

Sprinkle over the spring onions and serve the tofu with steamed rice. For a larger meal, add seared sweetheart cabbage and miso aubergine (eggplant).

# Spicy Miso Braised Leeks

●  ●
PREP:   COOK:
5 MINS  15 MINS

Though I'm an omnivore, I do love to take days off from eating meat. Before I embarked on this journey of recipe development and endless home cooking during the pandemic, I believed, like many others, that plant-based dishes were not as tasty or satisfying as those including meat. I now realize that this isn't true!

This braised leek dish is the perfect example of how amazing vegetables can be when made well. It is an absolute umami bomb and is now a regular on days when I seek to eat more veggies. If you're looking for an easy, flavour-packed, vegan-friendly dish, this is it.

- 500g (1lb 2oz) leeks, trimmed
- 2 tbsp cooking oil of choice

FOR THE BRAISING SAUCE
--------------------------------

- 2 garlic cloves, finely chopped
- 1 mild red chilli (chile), deseeded and finely chopped
- 1½ tbsp white miso paste (you could also use red miso paste or 2 tbsp light soy sauce)
- ½ tbsp sesame oil
- 1 tbsp (vegan) oyster sauce or mushroom stir-fry sauce
- 1 tbsp mirin

TO SERVE
--------------------------------

- ½ tsp toasted sesame seeds
- 1 tsp Easy Chilli Oil (see p.23)
- Steamed Rice (see p.21)

PAIRING SUGGESTIONS
--------------------------------

- Son-in-Law Eggs (see p.176)
- Easy Braised Pork Ribs (see p.66)

Slice the leeks in half widthways and then lengthways – you should have 4 long slices with a flat side to sear in a frying pan.

Combine the ingredients for the braising sauce in a bowl with 100ml (6½ tablespoons) of water and mix well. Set aside until later.

Heat the cooking oil in the largest frying pan you have (with a lid) on a high heat. Lay the slices of leek, flat-side down, in the pan and sear for about 2–3 minutes, until lightly browned.

Turn the heat down to medium and pour the braising sauce over the leeks. Cover with the lid and cook for 6–8 minutes, until the liquid has mostly evaporated.

Spoon the leeks onto a serving plate and top with the toasted sesame seeds and a drizzle of chilli oil and serve with steamed rice. The leeks are also delicious with son-in-law eggs and easy braised pork ribs.

BONUS

The hero here is miso, but I've also tried making it with soy sauce and it was just as good, although the sauce is slightly thinner in consistency.

# Kimchi Tofu Stew

PREP:
10 MINS

COOK:
10 MINS

Ever since a friend gave me a *ttukbaegi* - a traditional Korean earthenware pot - I've been making this recipe on repeat. I know you would traditionally make this ultra-comforting Korean dish with pork, but I really enjoy a meat-free version; the combination of soft silken tofu with the meaty texture of the shiitake mushrooms and crunch of the kimchi in a hearty, warming broth is quite perfect in my eyes. The fact that it also takes less than 30 minutes to prepare makes it ideal for a quick weeknight meal.

- 1 tbsp cooking oil of choice
- 1 tbsp gochugaru/Korean dried red chilli (chile) flakes
- ½ brown onion, finely sliced
- 3 garlic cloves, finely chopped
- 250g (9oz) kimchi, chopped, saving any juices
- 1 tbsp Korean gochujang paste (see p.13)
- 1 tbsp light soy sauce
- 1 tbsp sesame oil
- 4 shiitake mushrooms, sliced
- 300g (10oz) silken tofu, drained and diced
- 1 handful of chopped spring onions (green onions)
- Steamed Rice (see p.21), to serve, optional

PAIRING SUGGESTIONS
--------------------------------

- Korean Beef Bulgogi
  (see p.164)
- Kimchi Fried Rice
  (see p.116)

Heat the oil in a deep saucepan or *ttukbaegi* on a medium heat. Add the Korean chilli flakes, onion and garlic and sauté for 2 minutes, until fragrant.

Add the kimchi and any juices and stir to combine, followed by the gochujang paste, soy sauce, sesame oil and 500ml (generous 2 cups) of water. Mix to combine and to dissolve the paste.

Throw in the shiitake mushrooms, stir, then cover with a lid and simmer for 5 minutes.

Remove the lid and add the tofu to the pan, spoon over some of the sauce, cover again with the lid and simmer for another 2–3 minutes, until warmed through.

Sprinkle over the spring onions and remove the pan from the heat.

Serve over steamed rice or, for a Korean feast, with beef bulgogi and kimchi fried rice instead of plain steamed rice.

# Miso Aubergine

● ●
PREP: COOK:
5 MINS 40 MINS

This classic Japanese side dish combines a savoury umami-rich sauce with soft and silky fire-roasted aubergine (eggplant). I always used to order this dish (otherwise known as *nasu dengaku*) at Japanese restaurants, until I discovered it's super easy to make at home.

Traditionally, the recipe calls for Japanese aubergines, but they are not always an easy find, so I've used Italian aubergines instead. If you are able to grill these over a barbecue, then please do for that rich, smoky flavour but, if not, the oven works great as well. Both cooking methods will still result in a very delicious dish.

---

- 2 large aubergines (eggplants)

FOR THE MISO GLAZE
----------------------------------
- 1½ tbsp white miso paste
- 1 tbsp mirin
- ½ tbsp maple syrup
- ½ tsp sesame oil

TO SERVE
----------------------------------
- 1 tsp toasted sesame seeds, optional
- 1 tbsp finely chopped spring onion (green onion), optional
- Steamed Rice (see p.21)

PAIRING SUGGESTIONS
----------------------------------
- Garlic Broccoli (see p.76)
- Chinese Scrambled Eggs with Prawn (see p.62)

Preheat the oven to 200°C/180°C fan/400°F/Gas 6.

Slice the aubergines in half lengthways, then lightly score the flesh of each half in a criss-cross pattern. Place flesh-side up in a roasting tray.

Mix the ingredients for the miso glaze with 2 tablespoons of water in a bowl. Brush most of the glaze over the aubergine flesh, leaving some for later.

Place the roasting tray in the oven and cook the aubergines for 40 minutes, until they have browned and are soft to the touch.

Brush the aubergines with the remaining glaze. Sprinkle with sesame seeds and spring onions, if using, and serve alongside steamed rice with garlic broccoli and Chinese scrambled eggs with prawns (shrimp), if liked.

# Japchae

●          ●
**PREP:     COOK:**
**10 MINS*  10 MINS**

*plus pressing the tofu

This is another one of my absolute favourite Korean dishes. The simple and delicious combination of sesame oil, soy sauce and sugar is the reason why this sweet potato noodle dish is one of the most loved and sought after in Korean restaurants around the world.

Traditionally, each component in japchae is prepared individually, so that everything is seasoned well and texturally at an optimum. However, as I'm usually in a rush to eat when I'm hungry, my recipe is a quick alternative that can easily be adapted to suit whatever ingredients you have to hand.

---

- 250g (9oz) block of firm tofu, preferably smoked, drained
- 5-6 dried or fresh shiitake mushrooms
- 200g (7oz) sweet potato noodles
- 2 tbsp cooking oil of choice
- 2 garlic cloves, finely diced
- 1 brown onion, thinly sliced
- 100g (3½oz) king oyster mushrooms, thinly sliced
- 1 carrot, cut into julienne
- 1 large handful of chopped spring onions (green onions)
- 3 handfuls of spinach leaves
- 2 tsp toasted sesame seeds

## FOR THE STIR-FRY SAUCE

- 4 tbsp light soy sauce
- 2 tbsp sesame oil
- 1½ tbsp granulated sugar

## PAIRING SUGGESTIONS

- Chinese Scrambled Eggs with Prawn (see p.62)
- Dry Stir-Fried Green Beans (see p.53)

To remove any excess water in the tofu, wrap it in a few sheets of kitchen paper, place in a shallow dish and weigh down with heavy plates. Leave to drain for 30 minutes, then thinly slice.

Meanwhile, if you're using dried shiitake mushrooms, put them in a heatproof bowl and pour over enough just-boiled water from a kettle to cover. Leave to soak for 10 minutes, until rehydrated, then drain well. Thinly slice the rehydrated or fresh shiitake.

Mix all the stir-fry sauce ingredients together and set aside for later.

Cook the sweet potato noodles in a large pan of boiling water according to the packet instructions. Drain and rinse under cold running water. Using scissors, roughly cut the noodles into small pieces, then set aside.

Heat 1 tablespoon of the cooking oil in a large frying pan or wok on a medium–high heat. Add the tofu and stir-fry for 3-4 minutes, until lightly browned all over.

Make some space in the middle of the pan or wok, add the rest of the oil and sauté the garlic and onion for 1 minute. Throw in all the mushrooms and carrot and stir-fry for a further 1–2 minutes.

Turn the heat down to medium and toss in the cooked noodles, spring onions and spinach, then pour over the stir-fry sauce. Using tongs, combine everything together and cook until the sauce is absorbed and the spinach wilts.

Sprinkle with sesame seeds and serve on its own or with Chinese scrambled eggs and dry stir-fried green beans.

## Set Menu
.

→ SEARED SWEETHEART CABBAGE | 82

→ FISH-FRAGRANT AUBERGINE | 89

→ BLACK PEPPER TOFU | 90

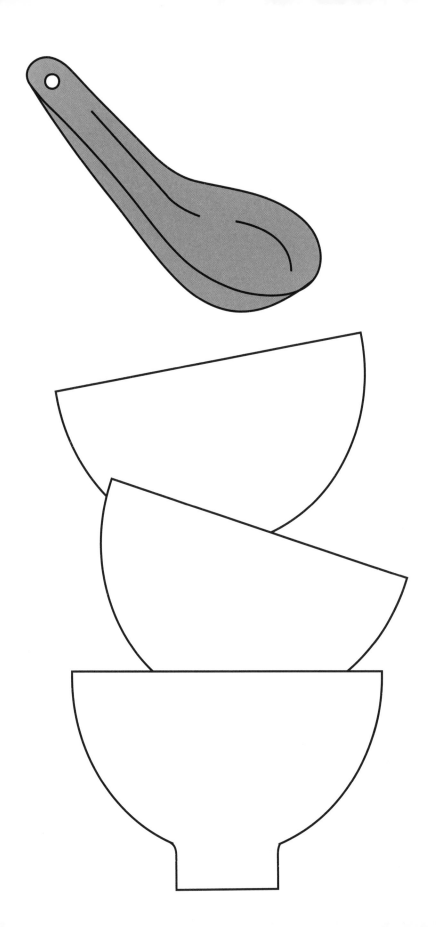

# Food for

# Comfort

# Food for Comfort

I hope these
dishes bring you
a sense of warmth
and love when
you're feeling
down or in need
of comfort.

My dad moved to the UK after my parents' divorce and two years later I joined him, leaving my life in China in March 2003. I landed with my first stepmum and her son at 6am on a red-eye flight from Hong Kong the following day. I still remember the first time I arrived at Canada Water station in southeast London, and the aroma of fresh pastries wafting from the small cafe by the ticket barrier. It was my first memory of food in the country I now call home. At that time, the 9-year-old me had no idea what the move meant or an understanding that familiar dishes made by my mum or grandma would become a thing of the past, or at the very least a rare treat on the odd occasion I went back to China to visit.

My father's second marriage didn't turn out to be all that great. My relationship with my stepmum at the time was also very problematic, and she often took her annoyance or anger with my dad out on me. I was frequently blamed and accused of things I didn't do. She also often told me that the reason why I was now with my dad was because my mum didn't want me; that I was unlovable, and that my dad had taken me on out of pity.

I never realized, until recently, how deeply this had damaged the way I perceived myself. Thank goodness for therapy. Back then, I was never taught how to regulate or express my emotions, so the way I learnt to deal with it all was through eating my feelings, and that included all kinds of junk food and sweet treats. Junk food wasn't something I was given when I lived with my grandparents in China, or when Mum was by my side; they were much more mindful of the things I ate as a child in terms of nutrition. But my new life in the UK meant that nothing was quite the same again.

For the next 4 years, that entire period of my life is empty in terms of food memories. In all honesty, I don't have much

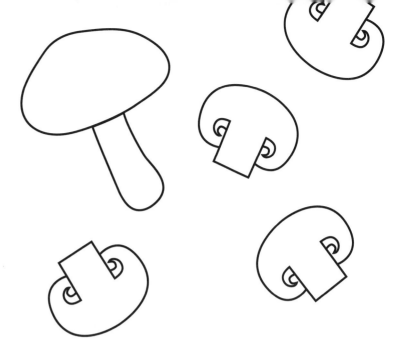

recollection of what we ate. All I know was that despite everything happening around me, it was reassuring that junk food was there for me and would never make me feel bad, even if I piled on a lot of weight. During those years, my turbulent childhood continued and became even worse at times, and I lost sight of what eating good food and being happy was all about.

Now, I didn't write this for sympathy; I wrote it because when trying to remember what meals I had eaten during those few years, my mind went completely blank. Absolutely nothing came to mind, apart from a few food-related incidents that were not happy memories at all. And it was an extraordinary realization that food is such a happy memory for me, so much so that my brain literally doesn't retain anything negative if it doesn't bring me joy.

In short, I did lose all the weight I had gained through many subsequent years of dieting, trying every method under the sun, and none of which I'd recommend to anyone. When I think about all those years spent counting calories and starving myself because society told me that I should be a certain size, I feel like I missed out on many opportunities to enjoy good food, that I will never get back.

Yet, this isn't a chapter based on diets or sad stories, it's about the meals that I have learned to cook subsequently; those that have given me a sense of comfort in a nourishing way. Some of these recipes slowly evolved into ones that brought me a feeling of stability and security because they were always reliably delicious, and nobody could argue otherwise. If, like me, you've had to go through some difficult times, I hope these dishes bring you a sense of warmth and love when you're feeling down or in need of comfort.

# Soothing Congee

**PREP:** **COOK:**
**5 MINS\*** **15 MINS\*\***

\*plus rehydrating mushrooms
\*\*if using uncooked rice,
the cooking time will be
1 hour, plus

A bowl of congee (soft cooked rice in a comforting broth) is a staple in many Asian households, particularly if you're a little under the weather. It is reputed to have healing powers as endorsed by all wise Asian grandmas and mums, including mine. Think of it as a sort of Asian version of risotto, or more accurately, a light savoury rice porridge - the real beauty of this dish is its simplicity. Rather than oats for breakfast, many Asian families welcome a bowl of warm rice congee, otherwise known as *jook* or *zhou* (粥), as their first meal of the day. I also, not-so-secretly, enjoy it as a light and comforting quick dinner

Congee is also super customizable to suit various dietary preferences and tastes, and it's worth checking out the many variations of the dish from different regions of China.

---

- 3 dried shiitake mushrooms
- 400g (3 cups) cooked short-grain rice (you can also make this with uncooked rice, but I find it easier to use leftover cooked rice)
- 2cm (¾in) piece of fresh root ginger, sliced
- 1 litre (4⅓ cups) vegetable stock or water

**FOR THE TOPPING (PER SERVING)**

--------------------------------

- 1 tbsp light soy sauce
- ½ tbsp Easy Chilli Oil (see p.23)
- ½ tsp sesame oil
- 1 handful of chopped spring onions (green onions) and/or coriander (cilantro)
- pinch of sesame seeds

To rehydrate the shiitake mushrooms, put them in a heatproof bowl and pour over enough just-boiled water from a kettle to cover. Leave to soak for 10 minutes, until rehydrated, then drain well and thinly slice.

In a small saucepan, add the cooked rice with the rehydrated shiitake, ginger and the vegetable stock or water. Bring to the boil, cover with a lid and simmer on a low heat for around 15 minutes, until the rice has softened and the liquid thickened.

Spoon the rice into two serving bowls. I like to season each serving with soy sauce, chilli oil, sesame oil, lots of spring onions and/or fresh coriander and sesame seeds, but you can definitely switch up the toppings to suit your preferences.

**BONUS**

Add your favourite protein for an extra flavourful bowl of congee - leftover cooked chicken, red meat or seafood work great here.

# Vegan Dan Dan Noodles

担担面

A popular Chinese street-food dish, dan dan noodles is widely known for its signature smoky, numbing and spicy flavour, thanks to the addition of Sichuan pepper.

Every bowl I've ever tasted comes with the chef's own interpretation and variations, and my version uses just vegetables, instead of the more traditional minced (ground) pork. The spicy sauce is so rich in umami that aubergines (eggplants) and mushrooms make the perfect vessel to absorb the distinctive flavours. This delicious noodle bowl also comes with pak choi (bok choy) instead of the more usual preserved mustard greens, which can be difficult to find. But, of course, if you do find the greens at your local Asian grocers, do use them for an authentic experience.

- ½–1 tbsp Sichuan peppercorns
- 2 tbsp cooking oil of choice
- 1 aubergine (eggplant), finely chopped
- 200g (7oz) chestnut mushrooms, finely chopped
- ½ tsp Chinese five-spice powder
- ½ tsp ground white pepper
- 1 tsp Chinese cooking wine
- 2 tsp hoisin sauce
- 1 tbsp light soy sauce
- 1 tbsp Sichuan Chilli Oil (see p.24)
- 1 handful of chopped spring onions (green onions)
- 200g (7oz) dried wheat noodles
- salt, to taste
- 5-6 pak choi (bok choy) leaves

FOR THE NOODLE SAUCE
- - - - - - - - - - - - - - - - - - - - - - - - - - - - - -
- 1 tbsp light soy sauce
- 1 tbsp Chinese black vinegar
- 1 tbsp smooth peanut butter
- 1 tbsp Sichuan Chilli Oil (see p.24)

TO SERVE
- - - - - - - - - - - - - - - - - - - - - - - - - - - - - -
- 1 tbsp crushed peanuts
- 1 tsp toasted sesame seeds
- 1 tbsp chopped spring onions (green onions)

Heat a small frying pan on a high, add the Sichuan peppercorns and toast for 2–3 minutes, tossing the pan occasionally. Once fragrant, tip the peppercorns into a bowl and set aside for later.

Heat the cooking oil in a large frying pan or wok on a medium–high heat. Add the aubergine and mushrooms and fry until browned and softened. Add all the seasonings and mix to combine. If it looks a little dry, add a splash of water to loosen and cook until the vegetables absorb most of the liquid. Throw in the spring onions towards the end and season with salt to taste – it may not need it.

Meanwhile, cook the noodles in a pan of boiling water according to the packet instructions. Drain and rinse under running cold water, then set aside.

In the same pan, bring some more water to the boil. Add the pak choi and blanch for 2 minutes, until just tender.

When everything is ready, mix all the ingredients for the noodle sauce in a large bowl. Add the cooked noodles, followed by the cooked aubergine and mushrooms.

Scatter over the crushed peanuts, sesame seeds and extra spring onions, and serve with the pak choi. Lightly toss everything together before enjoying.

# Red Braised Pork Belly

**PREP:**
15 MINS

**COOK:**
1 HOUR
15 MINS

This is my dad's favourite dish, so much so that he often requests it for his birthday meal, and I don't blame him. Chinese braised pork belly is beautiful in colour and melts in the mouth, thanks to the slow braising method. What's more, the deep-red hue of the pork is achieved through first caramelizing the sugar in oil before being used to coat the meat, hence the name red braised.

I would often accompany my grandma on shopping trips around the fresh markets and observe her fussing over the distribution of fat in the pork belly on display. She always demanded the pork be not too fatty or too lean, just somewhere in the middle.

When I make this dish, I like to serve it with some pickled vegetables. Since the pork is quite rich, the tangy freshness of the pickle brings a level of acidity and balance to the meal.

- 2 thick slices of fresh root ginger
- 2 spring onions (green onions), halved
- 500g (1lb 2oz) skin-on pork belly, chopped into 2.5cm (1in) cubes
- 1 tbsp cooking oil of choice
- 2 tbsp granulated sugar
- 1 star anise
- 2 tbsp light soy sauce
- 1 tbsp dark soy sauce
- 1 tbsp Chinese cooking wine
- Steamed Rice (see p.21), to serve

### PAIRING SUGGESTIONS
--------------------------------

- Pickled Cucumber (see p.27)
- Pickled Carrot & Daikon (see p.28)
- Sichuan Dry Pot Potatoes (see p.112)

Bring a large pan of water to the boil, then add the ginger, spring onions and pork belly. Turn the heat down slightly and simmer for 5 minutes, skimming off any impurities that rise to the surface. Turn off the heat, remove the pork belly with tongs and rinse under cold running water. Set aside and discard the contents of the pan.

Heat the cooking oil and sugar in a large saucepan on a high heat until the sugar melts and starts to caramelize, about 2–3 minutes.

Add the pork belly to the caramelized sugar, turn the meat to ensure it is thoroughly coated; this will give the pork the beautiful rich red colour.

Add the star anise, light and dark soy sauces and the Chinese cooking wine. Stir and pour in 1 litre (4⅓ cups) of water. Cover and simmer the pork for at least 45 minutes to 1 hour, stirring occasionally to prevent it burning and adding more water, if needed. You'll know the meat is ready when it's tender and soft, and the sauce has reduced and thickened.

Spoon the pork onto a serving plate and serve with some of the sauce spooned over accompanied by steamed rice and pickles. The pork is also delicious with Sichuan dry pot potatoes.

# Sichuan Dry Pot Potatoes

 干 锅 土 豆

● PREP: 10 MINS
● COOK: 15 MINS

In contrast to a hot pot - thinly cut meat and vegetables in a deliciously seasoned hot broth - another popular Sichuan-style of cooking is a dry pot, which avoids the use of liquid. Without water or stock, the spices and flavourings remain undiluted, which intensifies the flavour of whatever they are cooked with.

Potatoes, although plain in flavour when cooked on their own, take on an almost addictive quality when cooked in a dry pot with seasonings. I don't cook with potatoes that often, but when I do, it is most certainly this dish. If you're looking for ways to spice up your potato game, quite literally, this recipe might just be your new favourite way to enjoy spuds.

---

- 300g (10oz) white potatoes, peeled and cut into 1cm (½in) thick slices
- 3 tbsp cooking oil of choice
- ½ tbsp Sichuan peppercorns
- ½ brown onion, thinly sliced
- 3 garlic cloves, finely chopped
- 3-4 dried Sichuan chillies (chiles)
- 1 tbsp light soy sauce
- 1 heaped tbsp Chinese spicy bean paste (doubanjiang)
- 1 tbsp Sichuan Chilli Oil (see p.24)
- 1 tsp ground white pepper
- pinch of MSG, optional
- 1 handful of chopped spring onions (green onions)
- Steamed Rice (see p.21), to serve

### PAIRING SUGGESTIONS
----------------------------------

- Classic Egg-Fried Rice (see p.78)
- Easy Braised Pork Ribs (see p.66)

Place the sliced potatoes in a bowl filled with water and wash to rinse off the starch. Drain and pat dry with kitchen paper and set aside.

Heat 2 tablespoons of the cooking oil in a large frying pan or wok on a medium heat. Add the sliced potatoes and move them around to coat in the oil. Cook for around 5 minutes, turning the potatoes over halfway, until both sides are lightly browned. Remove from the pan with a slotted spoon and set aside.

In the same pan or wok, heat the remaining oil and add the Sichuan peppercorns and cook for 30 seconds, until fragrant. Add the onion and cook for 1 minute, until slightly softened. Next, add the garlic and toss for another 30 seconds.

Return the potatoes to the pan and stir-fry until the potatoes are cooked through. Toss in the dried chillies and add the soy sauce, spicy bean paste, chilli (chile) oil, pepper and MSG, if using, and ensure everything is thoroughly combined.

Throw in the spring onions just before turning off the heat. Toss through one last time and serve with steamed rice. Alternatively, serve with egg-fried rice and braised pork ribs.

# Kimchi Udon

● **PREP:** 10 MINS    ● **COOK:** 15 MINS

I love kimchi and I adore udon noodles, so it was a no-brainer to combine both foods in one fantastic meal. The slurpy texture of thick, chewy noodles with a sweet and savoury kimchi-flavoured sauce has me craving it, particularly after long trips to non-Asian countries; I always miss my dose of Asian cooking.

This dish is also very adaptable and you can easily turn it into a non-veggie meal by adding your favourite choice of protein, such as red meat, chicken or seafood. The fried egg is not essential either, if you want to keep it vegan friendly, but the runny yolk does add to the creaminess of the sauce, making it feel extra indulgent and luxurious. Oh, and by the way, this is great for a hangover!

---

- 200g (7oz) fresh udon noodles or 100g (3½oz) dried thick wheat noodles, cooked
- 2 tbsp cooking oil of choice
- 2 garlic cloves, finely chopped
- ½ shallot, finely chopped
- 1 tbsp Korean gochujang paste (see p.13)
- 80g (2¾oz) kimchi, roughly chopped
- ½ tbsp light soy sauce
- 1 tbsp honey or granulated sugar
- 1 handful of finely chopped spring onions (green onions)
- 1 fried egg, to serve, optional

Tip the fresh udon noodles into a large heatproof bowl and pour just-boiled hot water over to cover. Leave the noodles to soak for 10 minutes – this will help loosen them as they can be quite brittle. If using dried noodles, cook according to the packet instructions. Drain the noodles, saving 3 tablespoons of the water, and rinse briefly under cold running water before setting aside for later.

Meanwhile, heat the cooking oil in a frying pan or wok on a medium heat. Add the garlic and shallot and sauté for 2–3 minutes, until fragrant. Add the gochujang paste and kimchi and stir to combine.

Add the warmed or cooked noodles, followed by the soy sauce, honey or sugar and water from the noodles (or the tap), then stir through. Continue to cook for 3–4 minutes to allow the noodles to absorb some of the sauce. Lastly, toss in the spring onions and cook for another minute.

Plate up and serve topped with a fried egg, if you fancy an extra level of richness added by the yolk.

# Kimchi Fried Rice

● ●
PREP: COOK:
5 MINS 10 MINS

I know I've just included a recipe for Kimchi Udon (see p.114), but I love kimchi, so here's another great quick meal using the spicy fermented cabbage. This fried rice dish is a staple in Korean cooking and doesn't require many ingredients to make. I've also used Spam in my version - another popular ingredient in Korea - which was introduced by the US army during the Korean war in the 1950s. Spam (tinned cooked pork) became a feature of many dishes and recipes during that period when food was scarce, and meat even more so. It has since remained popular and Korea now manufactures tons of Spam, which actually differs from the type sold elsewhere due to the higher quantity and better quality of the meat used.

- 1 tbsp cooking oil of choice
- 2 garlic cloves, finely chopped
- 1 small brown onion, finely diced
- 1 tsp granulated sugar
- 1 tsp sesame oil
- 150g (5½oz) Spam, cubed
- 1 tbsp Korean gochujang paste (see p.13)
- 150g (5½oz) kimchi, roughly chopped, with any juices
- 400g (2 cups) cold cooked short-grain rice
- 1 handful of chopped spring onions (green onions)

TO SERVE (PER PERSON)
--------------------------------
- 1 fried egg
- ½ tsp toasted nori flakes
- ½ tsp toasted sesame seeds

PAIRING SUGGESTIONS
--------------------------------
- Korean Beef Bulgogi (see p.164)
- Soy & Garlic Tofu Bites (see p.46)

Heat the cooking oil in a large frying pan or wok on a medium heat. Once hot, add the garlic and cook for 30 seconds, until fragrant. Toss in the onion and cook for 2 minutes, until slightly softened.

Add the sugar, sesame oil, Spam, gochujang and kimchi, as well as any kimchi juices, and stir-fry for another 2–3 minutes, until thoroughly combined.

Mix in the cooked rice and heat through, stirring, until piping hot and combined. Toss in the spring onions, giving the rice one last stir, then remove from the heat.

Plate up and serve each portion topped with a fried egg, sprinkling of nori seaweed and sesame seeds. For a more substantial meal, serve with Korean beef bulgogi and soy and garlic tofu bites.

BONUS
Feel free to use smoked bacon instead of Spam, if preferred. Alternatively, make it vegetarian-friendly with cubes of smoked tofu.

# Honey Garlic Chicken

●     ●

**PREP:**    **COOK:**
15 MINS   40 MINS

This simple braised chicken is packed full of flavour, and regularly makes an appearance on my dinner table, especially during the week. I also make it in larger batches to portion into a lunchbox with rice, ready for a quick weekday meal - I'd be lying if I said I didn't get excited about lunch on those days. The combination of honey and garlic with a splash of vinegar gives the chicken a sweet and tangy flavour, which I just can't get enough of.

Braising is one of my favourite ways to cook since while the dish simmers, I can get on with preparing something else to go with it. Easy!

---

- ¼ tsp salt
- 1kg (2¼lb) skin-on boneless chicken thighs
- 4 garlic cloves, minced
- 1 brown onion, thinly sliced
- 350ml (1½ cups) chicken stock
- 3 carrots, about 200g (7oz), roughly chopped
- 1 handful of finely chopped spring onions (green onions)
- Steamed Rice (see p.21), to serve

**FOR THE SAUCE**
-------------------------------

- 2 tbsp runny honey
- 1 tbsp light soy sauce
- 1 tbsp rice vinegar or apple cider vinegar

**PAIRING SUGGESTIONS**
-------------------------------

- Spicy Miso Braised Leeks (see p.92)
- Egg Drop Soup (see p.38)

Sprinkle the salt over the chicken thigh fillets. Give it a good rub all over and leave the chicken to stand for 5–10 minutes while you prepare the rest of the ingredients.

Mix all the ingredients for the sauce together in a small bowl and set aside.

Heat a large sauté pan (with a lid) on a high heat. Place the chicken, skin-side down, in the pan and cook for 3–4 minutes, until some of the fat renders out and the skin becomes lightly browned. Flip the chicken over and cook for another 2–3 minutes, then remove from the pan. Keep any remaining oil in the pan.

In the same pan, now on a medium heat, add the garlic and sauté for 30 seconds. Add the onion and continue to cook for 2 minutes, stirring occasionally, until fragrant and translucent.

Return the chicken to the pan, pour in the stock, cover with the lid and simmer for 15 minutes, until the liquid has reduced by half.

Stir in the sauce prepared earlier. Add the carrots, cover and simmer for another 8–10 minutes, until the sauce has thickened but not completely evaporated, and the carrots are tender. Scatter over the spring onions and remove from the heat.

Serve the chicken with the sauce spooned over and steamed rice. This goes well with some spicy miso braised leeks and egg drop soup to turn this delicious meal into a feast.

# Sticky Cashew Tofu

●　　　●
PREP:　COOK:
15 MINS*　20 MINS

*plus pressing tofu

The thing with being Chinese and living outside my country of birth is that when I ask people what their favourite Chinese dish is, they sometimes name things I've never heard of. This was the case when I asked my American friend and she answered "cashew chicken". Turns out cashew chicken is a takeout dish popularized in the US and, when she realized I'd never had it before, she insisted we try it. Admittedly, the sticky savoury sauce with crunchy cashew nuts and tender chicken pieces was delicious - I couldn't help but enjoy it - so I've since recreated the dish a few times at home.

I also love it with tofu, as here. The pieces of tofu are coated in cornflour (cornstarch), pan-fried until crisp, then coated in a sticky sauce, so its texture kind of resembles chicken - well, at least to me!

---

- 350g (12oz) block of firm tofu, drained
- 50g (½ cup) cornflour (cornstarch)
- 3 tbsp cooking oil of choice
- 2 garlic cloves, minced
- 1 tsp finely chopped fresh root ginger
- 1 handful of roasted cashew nuts
- 1 handful of chopped spring onions (green onions)
- salt, to taste
- Steamed Rice (see p.21), to serve

FOR THE SAUCE
--------------------------------

- 2 tbsp light soy sauce
- 1 tbsp hoisin sauce
- 1 tbsp granulated sugar
- 2 tbsp rice vinegar

PAIRING SUGGESTIONS
--------------------------------

- Garlic Broccoli (see p.76)
- Crispy Sea Bass (see p.142)

To remove any excess water in the tofu, wrap it in a few sheets of kitchen paper, place in a shallow dish and weigh down with heavy plates. Leave to drain for 30 minutes, then cut or tear the tofu into bite-sized pieces.

Meanwhile, in a bowl, mix the ingredients for the sauce with 150ml (⅔ cup) of water and set aside.

Tip the cornflour into a shallow bowl. Press the tofu into the cornflour to generously coat all sides, then pat off any excess.

Heat 2 tablespoons of the cooking oil in a large frying pan on a medium heat. Add the tofu and gently fry, turning occasionally, until golden brown on all sides and there is no uncooked cornflour on the surface (you may need to cook the tofu in two batches). This takes around 10 minutes – if you rush it you may end up with floury tofu that's not very pleasant to eat.

When all the tofu is evenly browned, make some space in the middle of the pan and add the remaining cooking oil to sauté the garlic and ginger. Once fragrant, pour in the sauce and stir until the tofu is coated. Cook until the sauce thickens, becoming glossy and sticky.

Add the cashew nuts and spring onions and gently mix everything together one more time. Add salt, to taste. Dish up and serve with steamed rice as well as garlic broccoli. For a larger meal, accompany with crispy sea bass.

# Mapo Tofu

(麻)(婆)(豆)(腐)

**PREP:**
**10 MINS**

**COOK:**
**25 MINS**

Mapo tofu is a very popular Sichuan dish. The region is known for its spicy food, particularly dishes using Sichuan pepper, which gives any dish it touches the famous numbing or tingling spice sensation, also known as *mala* (麻辣), so it should come as no surprise to find that this dish is flavoured with the spice.

This dish certainly packs in the flavour - cubes of tofu (both silken and medium-firm tofu work here) are braised in a rich Sichuan pepper-spiced sauce with minced (ground) pork or beef and spring onions (green onions). If you're new to the sensation of *mala*, or prefer a milder-tasting dish, there are two ways to add the flavour of the pepper with varying results.

Traditionally, the freshly toasted Sichuan peppercorns are ground, then sprinkled over the dish so you get the *mala* sensation spread evenly throughout the meal. My personal preference though, as I'm somewhat wary of the numbing sensation, is to leave the peppercorns whole to infuse the oil, then pick them out before serving. But you can choose how to approach Sichuan peppercorns based on your taste preference.

This fabulous recipe can easily be made vegan, without taking away from the flavour of the dish, by swapping the minced meat for a plant-based alternative.

---

- 1 tbsp cooking oil of choice
- 1 tbsp Sichuan peppercorns
- 150g (5½oz) minced (ground) beef or pork, or plant-based alternative
- 3 garlic cloves, minced
- 1 tsp granulated sugar
- 1 heaped tbsp Chinese spicy bean paste (doubanjiang)
- 250ml (1 cup plus 1 tbsp) vegetable stock
- 300g (10oz) tofu (silken or medium-firm), drained and cut into bite-sized cubes
- ½ tbsp cornflour (cornstarch), optional

Heat the cooking oil in a large frying pan on a medium heat. Gently fry the Sichuan peppercorns for 2–3 minutes, tossing the pan occasionally, until fragrant and slightly darker in colour. If you prefer, remove the peppercorns from the oil at this stage. Leave them to cool, then grind in a pestle and mortar to sprinkle over at the end. Alternatively, keep the peppercorns whole in the pan.

To the same pan, add the mince and stir-fry for 4–5 minutes, until browned and the fat has rendered out.

Add the garlic and stir-fry for 30 seconds, until fragrant. Next, stir in the sugar, spicy bean paste and stock until combined. The sauce should be glossy and red with a nice sheen on top. Place the tofu on top and gently move it around so it's partially submerged in the liquid. Turn the heat down to low, cover with the lid and simmer for 5–10 minutes, until the sauce has slightly reduced.

- 1 handful of finely chopped spring onions (green onions)
- salt, to taste
- Steamed Rice (see p.21), to serve

PAIRING SUGGESTIONS
---------------------------------
- Lettuce in Oyster & Garlic Sauce (see p.56)
- King Prawns in Ginger & Garlic (see p.61)

Taste and adjust the seasoning, adding salt, if needed, or if it's too spicy, add a little extra sugar to balance out the flavour. If the sauce needs thickening, turn the heat up and simmer without a lid for a few more minutes until reduced. Alternatively, mix the cornflour with 2 tablespoons of water and add to the pan. Gently stir to combine, then simmer for a few minutes until thickened.

Toss in the spring onions and stir gently one last time until just wilted in the sauce. Sprinkle the ground Sichuan peppercorns over, if using, and serve the mapo tofu over steamed rice. For a more substantial meal, accompany with lettuce in oyster and garlic sauce and king prawns (shrimp) in ginger and garlic.

# Crispy Chicken & Leek Noodles

PREP:
15 MINS

COOK:
20 MINS

Imagine this… juicy, crispy-skinned chicken thighs on a bed of sweet leeks and noodles stir-fried in chicken juices. It's similar to the Shanghai Spring Onion Oil Noodles (see p.42), but enhanced with the flavour of chicken fat. The key to crispy-skinned chicken is to sear it, skin-side down, without moving to allow it to cook in the rendered-out fat. When you flip the chicken over, you should see a golden crisp skin that's guaranteed to be delicious.

The first time I made this umami-packed bowl, I just had to write down the recipe. I then made it several times over the following weeks and fed my nearest and dearest because feeding others is how I show my love. Watching them tuck in and fall in love with my food always makes my heart burst with joy.

---

- 3-4 skin-on boneless chicken thighs, depending on size
- 2 tbsp light soy sauce
- 100ml (6½ tbsp) vegetable stock
- 1 tbsp sesame oil
- 1 tbsp mirin
- 200g (7oz) dried wheat noodles (medium thick)
- 3 garlic cloves, minced
- 1 leek, thinly sliced
- salt, to taste

TO SERVE
------------------------------
- ½ tsp sesame seeds
- 1 handful of thinly sliced spring onions (green onions)
- 1 tsp Easy Chilli Oil (see p.23), optional

Pat dry the chicken skin with paper towels to remove any moisture. Sprinkle some salt on the other side, massage it in briefly and set aside for 10 minutes while you get on with the rest of the recipe.

Mix the soy sauce, stock, sesame oil and mirin in a bowl. Set aside.

Cook the noodles in a pan of boiling water according to the packet instructions. Drain and rinse under cold running water. Set aside.

Heat a large, dry frying pan on a medium–high heat. Place the chicken, skin-side down, in the pan and sear for 5–6 minutes, without moving the thighs, until browned. (You may want to cover the pan with a splatter screen to avoid any spitting oil.) Flip the chicken thighs over and cook for a further 3–4 minutes. Check that the chicken is cooked through and there is no trace of pink in the middle, then remove from the pan, saving the oil and juices.

To the pan, add the garlic and leek and stir-fry for 3–4 minutes, until fragrant and wilted. Toss in the soy sauce mixture, stir through and add the cooked noodles. Take care not to overcook the noodles to retain their texture. Taste and adjust the seasoning, if needed.

Remove from the heat and divide the noodles between two serving bowls. Slice the chicken thighs and place on top of the noodles. Top with toasted sesame seeds and spring onions, and a splash of chilli oil, if using.

# Steamed Scallops with Glass Noodles

粉 丝 蒸 扇 贝

**PREP:**
15 MINS

**COOK:**
10 MINS

At any Chinese family feast, you'll often spot one or two seafood dishes on the dining table, be it a steamed whole fish or a plate of shell-on prawns (shrimp). Seafood is always regarded as a sign of prosperity and good luck.

I know I use the word "favourite" a lot in this book, but this is hands down one of my favourite seafood dishes. Now that I'm older, I don't go home to see my family as often, but when I do and it's a celebratory occasion, I'm always excited to see if my dad has gone to the fish market to get some fresh scallops. As Dad always says, fresh seafood is best served steamed with minimal seasoning, so you can taste its natural flavour.

Here, the steamed scallops are served in a light sweet-and-savoury garlic sauce, which pairs perfectly with the natural sweetness of the seafood. The vermicelli noodles absorb the sauce beautifully too - everything about this dish just makes me salivate.

---

- 6 scallops, in the half shell
- 50g (1¾oz) dried mung bean vermicelli glass noodles
- ½ tbsp oyster sauce
- 2 tbsp light soy sauce
- ½ tbsp Chinese cooking wine
- ½ tbsp granulated sugar
- 1 tbsp cooking oil of choice
- 6 garlic cloves, minced
- 1 handful of chopped spring onions (green onions)

PAIRING SUGGESTIONS
--------------------------------
- Crispy Sea Bass (see p.142)
- Easy Braised Pork Ribs (see p.66)

To detach the scallops from their shells, carefully slice between where the scallop is attached and the shell, ideally as close to the shell as possible. Clean and wash the scallops. Score the top of each scallop with the tip of a pointed knife in a criss-cross pattern.

Put the vermicelli noodles in a heatproof bowl and pour over enough just-boiled water from a kettle to cover, then leave to soak for 10 minutes, until softened. Drain when ready.

Meanwhile, mix the oyster sauce, soy sauce, Chinese cooking wine and sugar together in a bowl.

Heat the cooking oil in a small saucepan on a low heat. Add the garlic and cook for 30 seconds, until fragrant. Pour in the sauce mixture and heat through, stirring until the sugar dissolves, then remove from the heat once ready.

Divide the vermicelli noodles between the shells, then place the scallops on top. Spoon the garlic sauce over and finish with a sprinkling of spring onions. Place the scallop shells on a plate or straight into a steamer and steam on a high heat for 6–8 minutes, depending on size, until tender and opaque in the centre. Serve piping hot. For a feast of a meal, enjoy with crispy sea bass and braised pork ribs.

SERVES 2

# Beef Ho Fun

●
PREP:
20 MINS

●
COOK:
10 MINS

If there's one dish I always order for dim sum it's this classic Cantonese-style beef stir-fry. Aside from the obvious myriad steamed dumplings and baos, it has become almost a ritual to order these smoky beef noodles.

If you've ever eaten a Chinese meat stir-fry, you may have wondered how it becomes so tender, and not chewy, after cooking. The secret is a method known as "velveting", and there are various ways to achieve this: some prefer to marinate the raw meat in a combination of egg white and cornflour (cornstarch), while others like to marinate it in bicarbonate of soda (baking soda) before rinsing and cooking the meat briefly in hot oil or water.

If you're curious, the rough science behind using cornflour is that it prevents the meat losing valuable moisture during cooking (leading to the protein strands tensing up) by acting as a barrier. This is why I also add cornflour to my scrambled eggs (see p.62). Similarly, adding bicarbonate of soda raises the surface pH of the meat, helping to prevent it becoming tough during cooking.

It's important to mix the cornflour or bicarbonate of soda into liquid before use as this allows them to coat each piece of meat evenly. If added dry, the powders will clump, making it impossible to get an even coverage.

- 1 tbsp cornflour (cornstarch)
- ¼ tsp bicarbonate of soda (baking soda)
- 2 tbsp cooking oil of choice, plus extra if needed
- 1 tsp Chinese cooking wine
- 1 tbsp light soy sauce
- 350g (12oz) sirloin or ribeye steak, thinly sliced on the diagonal
- 175g (6oz) dried wide flat rice noodles, or 350g (12oz) fresh rice noodles
- 1 small brown onion, thinly sliced
- 1 mild red chilli (chile), thinly sliced

In a shallow dish, mix together the cornflour, bicarbonate of soda, ½ tablespoon of the cooking oil, Chinese cooking wine and soy sauce. Add the steak, turn until coated all over and leave to marinate for 10–15 minutes while you carry on with the rest of the recipe.

To prepare the noodles, if using dried, cook them in a pan of boiling water for 1 minute less than the packet instructions as they will be cooked further later on. Drain and rinse under cold running water. Toss the noodles in 1 teaspoon of the cooking oil before setting aside – this will prevent them sticking together. If you manage to find fresh ho fun noodles, soak them in hot water before draining to gently separate the strands, then set aside; there is no need to coat them in oil.

Mix all the ingredients for the stir-fry sauce together and set aside. Heat 1 tablespoon of the cooking oil in a large frying pan or wok on a high heat. Add the marinated beef and stir-fry for 1 minute. Remove and set aside.

- 2cm (¾in) piece of fresh root ginger, peeled and thinly sliced
- 50g (1¾oz) beansprouts
- 1 handful of finely sliced spring onions (green onions)
- salt, to taste
- ½ tbsp Easy Chilli Oil (see p.23), to serve, optional

FOR THE STIR-FRY SAUCE
----------------------------------

- 100ml (6½ tbsp) beef stock
- ½ tbsp granulated sugar
- 1 tbsp oyster sauce
- 1 tsp dark soy sauce
- 1 tbsp light soy sauce

In the same pan or wok, turn the heat to medium–high and add a little more oil if needed. Add the onion, chilli and ginger and sauté for 2–3 minutes, until softened and fragrant.

Add the noodles and gently toss to break up any clumps. Stir in the stir-fry sauce and cook for another 2 minutes, until heated through and thoroughly combined.

Toss in the beef, beansprouts and spring onions and continue to stir fry for another 1–2 minutes, until softened a little. Taste and adjust the seasoning, adding salt, if needed. Dish up and serve piping hot with a splash of chilli oil, if using.

# Chinese Five-Spice Chicken

五香鸡腿

PREP:     COOK:
15 MINS*  30 MINS

*plus marinating

Another one of my top budget- and student-friendly dishes from university days. This five-spice chicken is super simple and packs in a ton of flavour. In fact, I'm pretty sure I made anyone I ever shared a kitchen with drool whenever I cooked this as it smells incredible. I give the credit to the five-spice with its fragrant combination of star anise, cloves, fennel, Chinese cinnamon (cassia) and Sichuan pepper. On top of that, the sweetness of the hoisin sauce and honey complements the savouriness of the soy sauce, and pairs particularly well with chicken.

For the best results, I get organized and marinate the chicken overnight - it's so worth it as the end result promises juicy, tender, umami-rich chicken with an irresistible glossy skin.

---

- 1kg (2¼lb) skin-on boneless chicken thighs
- Steamed Rice (see p.21), to serve

FOR THE MARINADE
--------------------------------
- 1 tbsp hoisin sauce
- 1 tbsp light soy sauce
- 1 tbsp runny honey or brown sugar
- 3 garlic cloves, minced
- 1 tsp Chinese five-spice powder
- 1 tsp dried chilli flakes (crushed red pepper flakes)

FOR THE SOY AND HONEY GLAZE
--------------------------------
- 1 tbsp light soy sauce
- 1 tbsp runny honey or maple syrup
- 1 tsp dark soy sauce

PAIRING SUGGESTIONS
--------------------------------
- Pickled Cucumber (see p.27) or Smacked Cucumber (see p.40)
- Chinese Tea Eggs (see p.32)

Mix all the ingredients for the marinade together in a shallow dish. Add the chicken thighs and turn until coated all over. Cover and leave to marinate for at least 2 hours or preferably overnight – the longer the better for maximum flavour.

When you're ready to cook, preheat the oven to 200°C/180°C fan/ 400°F/Gas 6 and line a roasting tray with aluminium foil to catch the juices while the chicken roasts. Remove the chicken from the marinade and place on a wire rack set over the lined tray. Pour over any remaining marinade juices.

Place the chicken in the oven and cook for 10–12 minutes, depending on the size of the thighs.

Mix all the ingredients for the soy and honey glaze together. Remove the chicken from the oven and brush the glaze all over, then return to the oven for another 5–7 minutes, until cooked through and golden. (If using bone-in chicken thighs, cook them for 25–30 minutes in total.)

To help crisp up the skin, turn the oven to the grill (broiler) function and cook for a final 5 minutes. The chicken should be sizzling, golden and glossy in appearance when ready.

Allow the chicken to rest for a few minutes for ultimate juiciness before serving. Slice and serve with steamed rice, pickled or smacked cucumber and halved Chinese tea eggs.

# Set Menu

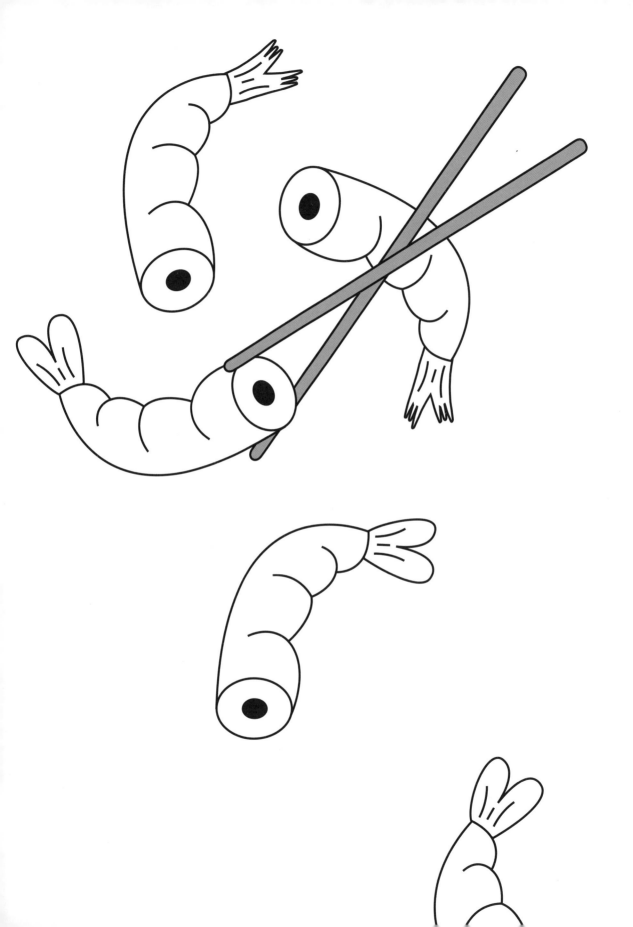

# Food for

# Reminiscing

# Food for Reminiscing

Growing up, I
developed a thirst
for exploring new
places. For years,
I'd watched
cooking and food
programmes…
and I dreamt
longingly of
one day visiting
these countries…

My dad divorced my first stepmum when I was about fourteen, and a year later he remarried again. My current stepmum is more like an older sister to me than a mother and I love that – I'd never really experienced having siblings in my life and I was always envious of friends who had brothers and sisters growing up.

To cut a very long story short, Dad and my stepmum now have three sons, which means I have three half-brothers and they're great because they're like my minions, in the best possible way!

I'd like to think I'm a good influence on them, she says modestly, especially when it comes to travelling and exploring the world. The eldest of the three is Feifei (a nickname), who is fourteen at the time of writing, and already taller than me. He loves hearing about my travel stories, and I love showing him pictures of places I've been to and the food I've enjoyed. My other two half-brothers, who are ten and eight, are also interested, but more so in the activities I get up to, like diving, surfing or anything adventurous.

(By the way, my mum also remarried to my current stepdad, who is lovely, and because he'd never had a child, they both treat me like a princess whenever I go home to Shanghai to visit. He once told me how it's as if he skipped the tough part of bringing up a child and just went straight to the grown-up stage, when that child has her life sorted.)

Growing up, I developed a thirst for exploring new places. For years, I'd watched cooking and food programmes showcasing all kinds of international cuisines, and I dreamt longingly of one day visiting these countries, so I could experience them for myself. So, as soon as I had some kind of financial independence, I booked flights to almost anywhere and everywhere, whenever possible.

For me, there's no better way to get to know a place than by enjoying some of the most loved local delicacies, however different they may be to my own. I started by exploring countries close to the UK, first western Europe – France, Spain, Italy – and then ventured slowly eastwards, including the Czech Republic, Hungary and Poland which, incidentally, was where I discovered dishes that bare similarities to those served in Asian cuisines. Many trips were solo, and they turned out to be some of my favourite places and experiences ever.

At the risk of sounding like every other gap-year backpacker, travelling to Southeast Asia by myself was life changing. My first experience of Thailand was an intense sensory stimulation: the humidity, the warmth, the people, the endless streets lined with food trucks, and home cooks selling what they do best. I wasn't so interested in restaurant-dining experiences, I always just followed the locals – if there was a line of people queueing to eat, this was often a good sign. Even the hot food served at convenience stores was delicious.

This was also the case in Vietnam, where I went for a three week adventure. I'd already be deciding on what was going to be my next meal as I tucked into breakfast. I also tried to make it my mission to learn the secret or back-story to each delicious dish by asking the food stall owner for cooking tips.

It never occurred to me before the coronavirus pandemic in 2020 that thanks to my travelling experiences, I was able to recreate lots of my favourite dishes at home. When I miss my solo adventures, I often reminisce about those days by cooking something that makes me smile and brings back great memories!

SERVES 2

# Bún Chả

My obsession with this Vietnamese noodle dish is immeasurable. Even before I travelled to the country, every time I went to a Vietnamese restaurant in London, I'd always order bún chà, and it may come as a surprise, but I prefer it over the other famous Vietnamese dish, phô, particularly the way the zingy noodle salad unites many of my favourite components of Vietnamese cooking in one dish. The nuoc cham dressing with its balance of tangy fish sauce, sour lime juice, chilli (chile) heat and sweetness of the sugar, brings everything together.

- 1 tbsp cooking oil of choice
- 150g (5½oz) dried vermicelli rice noodles
- 1 handful of lettuce leaves, such as Little Gem or romaine, roughly chopped
- 1 small red chilli (chile), finely chopped
- 1 handful of fresh coriander (cilantro), chopped
- 50g (1¾oz) Pickled Carrot & Daikon (see p.28)
- 2-3 lime wedges

## FOR THE MEATBALLS

- 350g (12oz) minced (ground) pork
- 2 garlic cloves, minced
- 1 handful of chopped spring onions (green onions)
- 1 lemongrass stalk, outer layer removed, inside finely chopped
- 1 tbsp fish sauce
- ½ tbsp granulated sugar
- ½ tsp ground white pepper
- ½ tsp salt

## FOR THE NUOC CHAM

- 2 garlic cloves, minced
- 1 red chilli (chile), finely chopped
- 1 tbsp granulated sugar
- 1 tbsp fish sauce
- 1 tbsp rice vinegar
- 1 tbsp lime juice

To prepare the meatballs, put all the ingredients in a large bowl and stir continuously in one direction for about 5 minutes, until combined. Using your hands, shape the mixture into 10 equal-sized small meatballs.

Heat the cooking oil in a large frying pan or griddle on a medium heat. Add the meatballs and cook, turning occasionally and pressing to flatten slightly, until slightly charred on the outside and cooked through on the inside. This should take 6–8 minutes.

Meanwhile, prepare the vermicelli rice noodles according to the packet instructions. Drain and rinse under cold running water for 30 seconds, then divide between two serving bowls.

Mix all the ingredients for the nuoc cham with 5 tablespoons of water in a bowl and set aside.

To assemble the bún chà, place the meatballs on top of the cooked vermicelli noodles in the serving bowls, add the lettuce leaves, chilli, coriander and pickled carrot and daikon. Spoon the nuoc cham dressing on top and squeeze over the lime juice, then mix gently to combine.

FUN FACT

I'm not the only person who loves bún chà, the recipe also proudly made it into *The Platinum Jubilee Cookbook* in 2022. Great minds dine alike, I'd say!

# Beijing Zhajiangmian

PREP:
10 MINS

COOK:
20 MINS

The literal translation of *zhajiangmian* is "fried sauce noodles", and this simple, popular dish of noodles with fatty pork, stir-fried in a savoury and umami-packed dark soybean sauce originates from northern China. I first tried it when I went to Beijing in 2012, where it's arguably so well known that the name of the city is almost always part of the title of the dish.

I'll be the first to admit that this version is not the most authentic as I've simplified it a little using ingredients that can be more easily found outside of China. To be precise, I've replaced the original *tian mian jiang* (甜面酱), or sweet bean sauce, with the more readily available hoisin sauce, since their flavour profiles are quite similar.

- 2 tbsp cooking oil of choice
- 150g (5½oz) minced (ground) pork
- 1 small onion, finely diced
- 3 garlic cloves, minced
- 2cm (¾in) piece of fresh root ginger, finely chopped
- 2 tbsp ground soybean paste
- 1 tbsp hoisin sauce
- ½ tbsp dark soy sauce
- 1 tsp Chinese cooking wine
- 100g (3½oz) dried wheat noodles (medium)
- 1 spring onion (green onion), finely chopped

TO SERVE

- 40g (1¾oz) cucumber, cut into julienne strips
- 40g (1¾oz) Pickled Carrot & Daikon (see p.28)

PAIRING SUGGESTION

- Garlic Broccoli (see p.76)

Heat the cooking oil in a large frying pan or wok (with a lid) on a medium–high heat. Add the minced pork and stir-fry for 3–4 minutes to render out some of the fat and until the meat is lightly browned.

Add the onion, garlic and ginger and stir-fry for a further 1–2 minutes, until fragrant and slightly softened.

Add the soybean paste, hoisin sauce, soy sauce and Chinese cooking wine. Pour in 150ml (⅔ cup) of water and stir to combine. Cover with the lid and simmer on a low heat for 10 minutes, until most of the liquid has evaporated.

Meanwhile, cook the noodles in a pan of boiling water according to the packet instructions. Drain and refresh under cold running water and place in a serving bowl.

Once the sauce is ready, taste and add salt, if needed. Throw in the spring onion and stir through one last time. Remove from the heat and spoon the sauce over the noodles.

Serve with a side of freshly sliced cucumber and pickled carrot and daikon. A serving of garlic broccoli also makes a good accompaniment. Enjoy!

# Crispy Sea Bass

●       ●

PREP:     COOK:
5 MINS   10 MINS

A whole steamed sea bass served topped with thin slices of spring onion (green onion) and ginger with a drizzling of hot sesame oil is a popular offering in Chinese homes and restaurants. The aroma is divine and it's one of my all-time favourite fish dishes in the world. Remember when I mentioned how my parents frequently sold me the idea that eating more fish would make me smarter? Well, I was fed this many times over growing up.

For the purpose of ease of preparation and cooking, I've used sea bass fillets instead of a whole fish. Let's be honest, I never paid much attention to my dad's many attempts to teach me how to scale and gut fish.

---

- 2 sea bass fillets, about 200g (7oz) total weight, skin-on and bones picked out
- 2 tbsp cornflour (cornstarch)
- 2 tbsp cooking oil of choice
- 20g (¾oz) fresh root ginger, peeled and cut into thin matchsticks
- 3 spring onions (green onions), finely sliced into thin strips
- 2 tbsp light soy sauce
- ½ tbsp sesame oil
- Steamed Rice (see p.21), to serve

PAIRING SUGGESTIONS
----------------------------------

- Sticky Cashew Tofu (see p.120)
- Seared Sweetheart Cabbage (see p.82)

Pat dry the sea bass fillets with kitchen paper to remove as much moisture as possible – this will ensure the skin turns ultra crispy when fried.

Put the cornflour in a shallow dish. Lay the sea bass in the cornflour and turn to coat both sides, then pat off any excess.

Heat half the oil in a small frying pan on a medium heat. Add the ginger and spring onions and cook for a couple of minutes until fragrant. Add the soy sauce and sesame oil and cook for another minute. Remove from the heat and set aside.

In a large frying pan, heat the remaining cooking oil on a high heat.

Lay the sea bass, skin-side down, in the pan and cook for around 2–3 minutes, pressing the fish down with a spatula to make sure the skin maintains contact with the pan to achieve ultimate crispness. Turn the fish over and cook for another minute or two until the fish is cooked and golden in places.

Place the fish on serving plates, drizzle the ginger and spring onion sauce over and serve with steamed rice. Alternatively, enjoy the sea bass as part of a larger meal with sticky cashew tofu and seared sweetheart cabbage.

# Sizzling Pepper Rice

**PREP:**
**10 MINS**

**COOK:**
**20 MINS**

During a short visit to Tokyo, Japan, I slurped on numerous bowls of ramen, and snacked on many different onigiris from convenience stores. I also dined at the restaurant chain, Pepper Lunch, after spotting a long line of Japanese salarymen queuing to eat there - always a good sign. If you haven't come across Pepper Lunch before, it's well-known for its DIY restaurant concept of cook-your-own sizzling steak in a hot cast-iron pan. The sliced beef comes with a generous serving of garlic butter alongside a scoop of sweetcorn. A mound of fluffy steamed Japanese rice is, of course, mandatory too, but most importantly, the sweet tangy sauce is really the hero that brings it all together.

Here's my recreation of that Japanese dish, and it's a veggie version too. Feel free to add in slices of beef, if you like though.

---

- 140g (1 cup) Japanese short-grain rice, rinsed well
- 2 tbsp cooking oil of choice, plus extra for the rice
- 1 red bell pepper, deseeded and thinly sliced
- 100g (3½oz) sweetheart cabbage, thinly sliced
- 250g (9oz) chestnut mushrooms, thinly sliced
- ¼ tsp salt
- 100g (3½oz) sweetcorn kernels, canned or frozen
- 1 tbsp vegan butter

FOR THE SAUCE
---------------------------------

- 2 tbsp light soy sauce
- 1 tbsp maple syrup
- ½ tsp MSG, optional
- ½ tbsp cornflour (cornstarch)

Cook the rice according to the instructions on the packet.

Meanwhile, put all the ingredients for the sauce and 75ml (5 tablespoons) of water in a small frying pan, stir and heat gently until thickened. Remove and set aside.

Heat the cooking oil in a large cast-iron pan on a medium heat. Once hot, add the red pepper and sauté for 2–3 minutes, until slightly softened. Next, add the cabbage, mushrooms and salt, and continue to sauté for 2–3 minutes, until softened. Lastly, stir in the sweetcorn until combined and cook for another minute.

Once the rice is cooked, spoon it into a medium-sized bowl and press down with the back of a spoon until the top has flattened.

Move the vegetables to the edges of the pan to make space for the rice in the middle. Add a little more oil to the middle of the pan and tip the rice in the bowl upside down into the space, then carefully lift off the bowl – you should have a dome of rice. Place the butter on top of the rice.

To serve, drizzle the sauce over the rice and vegetables. Serve immediately from the pan. It is best enjoyed when the rice, vegetables and sauce are mixed together before eating.

# Taiwanese Beef Noodle Soup

●　　　●
PREP:　COOK:
10 MINS　20 MINS

I firmly believe that a bowl of warming and flavour-packed noodles is what dreams are made of. You've probably noted by now that I also love all kinds of noodle soup, and when I visited Taiwan a few years back I spent many days sampling the different ones the country had to offer.

This beef noodle soup (originally brought to the island by Chinese civil war refugees to remind them of a taste of home) was right up there with the best. During my visit, my favourite bowls of this soup were served in restaurants where you share a table, rubbing elbows with fellow diners. I remember, there was always a hum of enjoyment as steam diffused into the room from the adjoining kitchen, with pots of slowly braised meat simmering away next to pans of richly spiced broth.

Not everyone has hours on hand to slow-cook beef brisket though, so I have come up with this cheat's version using frozen hot-pot beef slices. Available from Chinese supermarkets, the thinly cut beef takes mere seconds to cook from frozen in the hot broth, and the marbling always promises delicious tender meat. This hearty and spicy beef broth also comes with chewy noodles and is finished off with a handful of fresh spring onions (green onions) and coriander (cilantro) and is nothing short of satisfying.

- 200g (7oz) dried wheat noodles (thin or medium)
- 2 pak choi (bok choy), sliced in half lengthways
- 200g (7oz) frozen beef slices

FOR THE BROTH
-----------------------------------
- 2 tbsp cooking oil of choice
- 3cm (1¼in) piece of fresh root ginger, thinly sliced
- 3 garlic cloves, crushed
- 1 brown onion, roughly chopped
- 2 large tomatoes, roughly chopped

To make the broth, heat the cooking oil in a large pot on a medium heat. Add the ginger, garlic and onion and stir-fry for 2–3 minutes, until fragrant and slightly softened.

Add the tomatoes and cook for another minute, then add the spicy bean paste and Chinese five-spice and mix to combine. Add the rest of the ingredients for the broth to the pot with 1 litre (4⅓ cups) of water and bring to the boil.

Turn the heat to medium–low and maintain a gentle simmer with the lid on for 15 minutes, until the tomatoes start to break down and thicken the soup slightly. Taste and add salt to taste.

While the soup simmers, bring a separate pot of water to the boil and cook the noodles according to the packet instructions. At the same time, steam the pak choi until tender.

- 2 tbsp Chinese spicy bean paste (doubanjiang)
- 1 tsp Chinese five-spice powder
- 1 tbsp light soy sauce
- 1 tsp Chinese cooking wine
- 1 beef stock cube
- salt, to taste

TO SERVE
----------------------------------

- 1 handful of fresh coriander (cilantro), roughly chopped
- 1 handful of finely chopped spring onions (green onions)
- Easy Chilli Oil (see p.23), optional

Drain and refresh the noodles under cold running water. Divide the noodles between two serving bowls and top with the cooked pak choi, then set aside.

Once everything is prepared, return the broth to the boil (topping up with more water, if needed). Add the frozen beef and cook until it is no longer pink in appearance - this should take no more than a minute. Remove the pot from the heat and ladle the beef and broth into the bowls with the noodles and pak choi.

Finish off with a sprinkling of coriander and spring onions and a drizzle of chilli oil, if you like it more spicy.

# Spiced Lamb Soup Noodles

**PREP:**
10 MINS

**COOK:**
30 MINS

In the city of Xi'an, where my stepdad is from, comes this hearty and comforting lamb soup served with shredded flatbreads, which are soaked in the spiced broth.

Once, after returning to China for the Lunar New Year, I suggested to my Shanghai parents (my mum and stepdad) that we take a trip to Xi'an as I had never been there before. The weather there was bitterly cold and, wrapped in thick layers, we wandered around looking for food and warmth. My stepdad led us to a plain wooden door and once inside we discovered this steam-filled room with tables of hungry diners slurping away on bowls of soup. We sat down at a table and the waiter strolled over to ask us how many we'd like. My stepdad gestured two, which he said was plenty for all three of us, and the waiter brought us two empty bowls and two flatbreads. My mum and stepdad began to tear the bread apart and put it into the bowls, so I joined in, curious to find out what was going to happen next. Before I could ask, the waiter took the bowls away before returning with them filled with a steaming broth ladled over the torn-up flatbreads; it was the perfect dish to eat on a bitterly cold day.

Inspired by the memory of that meal, and feeling slightly homesick, I have recreated the lamb soup, but using mung bean vermicelli noodles instead of flatbreads.

- 5g dried wood ear mushrooms
- 1 tsp cumin seeds
- 200g (7oz) minced (ground) lamb, ideally 20% fat
- 3cm (1¼in) piece of fresh root ginger, peeled and minced
- 3 garlic cloves, minced
- 2-3 dried Chinese chillies (chiles), deseeded and chopped
- 1 tbsp light soy sauce
- 750ml (3 cups) lamb stock
- 1 small stick Chinese cinnamon (cassia), about 5cm (2in) long

Place the dried wood ear mushrooms in a small bowl and pour over just-boiled water. Set aside while you prepare everything else.

Heat a small dry frying pan on a medium heat. Add the cumin seeds and toast for 3–4 minutes, tossing occasionally to prevent them from burning. Once fragrant and slightly darker in colour, remove and set aside.

Heat a large dry frying pan on a medium heat. Once hot, add the minced lamb and cook for 6–7 minutes, stirring often, until browned and some of the fat has rendered out. Move the lamb aside to make space in the middle of the pan. Add the ginger, garlic and dried chilli to the pan and sauté in the oil from the lamb for 2–3 minutes, until fragrant. Stir in the soy sauce until combined. Strain the mixture through a sieve to separate the juices. Place the mince in a bowl and set aside for later.

- 1 bay leaf
- 1 star anise
- 200g (7oz) dried mung bean
  vermicelli noodles
- 1 pak choi (bok choy),
  halved lengthways
- 100g (3½oz) frozen lamb
  slices

## TO SERVE

- 1 handful of finely chopped
  spring onions (green
  onions)
- 1 handful of coriander
  (cilantro), roughly chopped
- ¼–1 tbsp Sichuan Chilli Oil
  (see p.24), optional

## PAIRING SUGGESTION

- 2 Japanese Soy-Marinated
  Eggs (see p.31)

Pour the strained juices into a pan with the stock. Throw in the cinnamon stick, bay leaf, star anise and toasted cumin seeds. Bring to a gentle boil, then turn the heat down to low and simmer for 15 minutes.

Meanwhile, bring a pot of water to the boil and cook the noodles according to the packet instructions. Once cooked, drain and rinse briefly under cold running water. Divide the noodles between two serving bowls.

While the noodles are cooking, blanch the pak choi in a separate pan of boiling water for 1–2 minutes, until just tender. Drain and place on top of the noodles when ready. Drain the soaked wood ear mushrooms and place on top of the noodles too.

Return the broth to the boil (topping up with more water, if needed). Add the frozen lamb and cook until it is no longer pink in appearance – this should take no more than a minute. Remove the pot from the heat and ladle the lamb and broth into the serving bowls over the noodles, pak choi and mushrooms.

Spoon the cooked mince mixture over and scatter with the spring onions and coriander before serving. If you like, enjoy with a spoonful of chilli oil and a soy-marinated egg on the side.

BONUS

I've used vermicelli noodles here, but you could also use sweet potato noodles (see p.17) if you prefer a slightly thicker noodle with a chewier texture.

SERVES 2

# Char Sīu
## (Chinese BBQ Pork)

叉烧

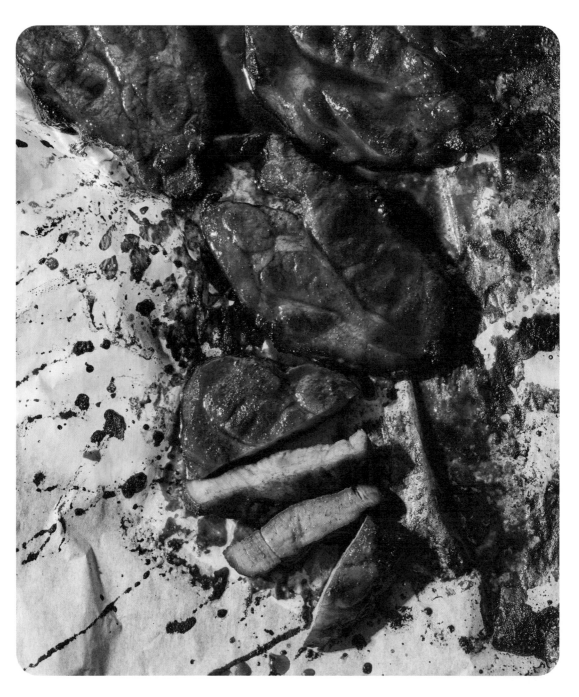

One of the most-loved dishes from Guangdong Province, this Canton-style pork is traditionally skewered onto long forks and roasted over fire, which gives it the name *char siu* (in Cantonese) or *cha shao* (in Mandarin), which both translate as "fork roasted". The taste of the roasted pork is a delicate balance of sweet and savoury, with Chinese spices and charred barbecued bits.

It is common to see rows of char siu pork, with its signature red hue, hanging in the windows of roasted meat shops in the city of Guangzhou as well as Hong Kong. You're likely to spot it hanging alongside whole roasted ducks, which are equally as eye-catching with their glistening skin, but that's a recipe for another time.

Back to the glorious barbecue pork… I discovered during the lockdowns of 2020 that it was actually quite easy to recreate a similar dish at home. The red hue is traditionally achieved using fermented red bean curd, but when I made it without, the result still tasted fantastic. I have since added red food colouring in an attempt to achieve the aesthetic of restaurant-style char siu, but you can definitely skip it, if preferred.

---

- 600g (1lb 5oz) pork fillet or thick pork shoulder steaks
- 3 tbsp light soy sauce
- 4 tbsp runny honey
- ½ tbsp soft light brown sugar
- 2 tbsp hoisin sauce
- 1 tsp Chinese five-spice powder
- ⅛ tsp red food colouring, optional

## TO SERVE

- Steamed Rice (see p.21)
- blanched leafy green vegetables, such as pak choi (bok choy)

## PAIRING SUGGESTIONS

- Garlic Broccoli (see p.76)
- Classic Egg-Fried Rice (see p.78)
- Wonton Noodle Soup (see p.202)

Prick the pork fillet or shoulder all over with a fork to help the marinade penetrate the meat. Place in a ziplock bag or container.

In a bowl, mix together the soy sauce, 3 tablespoons of the honey, the sugar, hoisin sauce, Chinese five-spice and food colouring, if using, until combined. Reserve 2 tablespoons of the marinade in a separate bowl to be used for basting later. Pour the rest into the bag or container with the pork. Turn to coat the pork in the marinade, then seal and leave to marinate in the fridge for at least 3–4 hours, preferably overnight.

When ready to cook, preheat the oven to 220°C/200°C fan/425°F/Gas 7 and line a roasting tin with foil to catch any juices. Put the pork on a wire rack over the roasting tin and brush with any marinade left in the bag or container. Roast for 40–45 minutes.

Mix the reserved marinade in the bowl with the remaining honey and brush this all over the pork at 10-minute intervals, turning the meat over occasionally to make sure all sides are basted. After 45 minutes, check if the pork is cooked (the internal temperature should read 68°C/155°F with a meat thermometer) and the outside caramelized slightly with charred bits. If not, place the pork under a high grill for a further 5–8 minutes, watching it closely as it caramelizes to make sure it doesn't burn.

Remove from the oven or grill and brush the pork one last time with any remaining marinade. Allow the pork to rest for 5 minutes before slicing and serving with steamed rice and a leafy vegetable of your choice. It's also delicious served with garlic broccoli, classic egg-fried rice and wonton noodle soup.

# Thai Pineapple Fried Rice

**PREP:**
**15 MINS***

**COOK:**
**10 MINS**

Apart from pad Thai, one of the first meals I ate while in Thailand was pineapple fried rice. I had never eaten fried rice flavoured with curry powder before, but it was really delicious and worked surprisingly well with the sweet juiciness of the pineapple. Now, every time I make this, I feel like I'm back on holiday in Thailand, especially if I enjoy it with a cold beer on the side.

- 3 tbsp cooking oil of choice
- 2 large eggs, whisked
- 1 brown onion, finely chopped
- 350g (2½ cups) cold cooked Thai jasmine rice
- 100g (3½oz) raw king prawns (shrimp), peeled and deveined
- 100g (3½oz) frozen or fresh vegetable medley, such as peas and carrots
- 200g (7oz) ready-prepared fresh pineapple pieces, cut into small cubes
- 2 tbsp light soy sauce
- 1 tbsp fish sauce
- ½ tbsp curry powder
- 1 tsp ground white pepper
- 1 handful of thinly sliced spring onions (green onions)

Heat 1 tablespoon of the cooking oil in a large frying pan on a medium heat. Pour in the eggs and cook gently, moving and turning them until scrambled. Roughly break up any large pieces of egg when cooked, then remove from the pan and set aside.

In the same frying pan, heat another 1 tablespoon of the cooking oil and add the onion. Sauté for several minutes until translucent.

Stir in the rice until combined and heat through thoroughly, then make a space in the middle of the pan and add the rest of the oil. Throw in the prawns and cook for 2–3 minutes, until pink.

Gradually add the vegetables, pineapple, soy sauce, fish sauce, curry powder and white pepper. Stir to combine everything and heat through, then fold in the spring onions and cooked egg. Spoon into a bowl and serve on its own, or with some crispy sea bass and spring rolls for a larger meal.

**PAIRING SUGGESTIONS**

- Crispy Sea Bass (see p.142)
- Classic Spring Rolls (see p.174)

**BONUS**

I sometimes like to serve the rice in a pineapple bowl made from the hollowed-out fruit - for me, it adds to the ambience of the dish. To prepare, take a ripe pineapple and stand it upright on a board. Cutting downwards, slice off a third of the fruit, leaving the main part with the leaves attached. Cut out the fruit from the smaller piece and discard the skin. To remove the fruit from the larger piece, cut horizontal and vertical lines to make a grid, leaving a 3cm (1¼in) shell. Scoop out the fruit and cut into small cubes, discarding the hard core and leaving a bowl-shaped shell.

# Spicy Thai Basil Pork
## (Pad Kra Pao Moo)

●
PREP:
10 MINS

●
COOK:
10 MINS

Before travelling to Thailand, I knew very little about the country's food, aside from pad Thai and Thai green curry. During my solo adventure to the country in 2018, I ordered this pork dish after seeing someone else tucking into it on the table next to me. I fell completely in love with this spicy stir-fry - one of the most popular dishes in Thailand.

Made with minced (ground) pork, Thai basil (Italian basil can be used as a substitute), chillies (chiles) and garlic, and served over rice with a crispy fried egg on top, it is an absolute banger of a quick meal.

- 1 tbsp cooking oil of choice
- 2 garlic cloves, finely chopped
- 2 bird's eye chillies (chiles), deseeded and finely chopped
- 300g (10oz) minced (ground) pork
- 1 large handful of Thai basil, roughly chopped

### FOR THE STIR-FRY SAUCE

- 1 tbsp light soy sauce
- 1 tbsp oyster sauce
- 1 tbsp fish sauce
- ½ tsp dark soy sauce
- ½ tbsp granulated sugar

### TO SERVE

- 2 fried eggs, optional
- Steamed Rice (see p.21)

### PAIRING SUGGESTIONS

- Pickled Carrot & Daikon (see p.28)
- Egg Drop Soup (see p.38)

In a small bowl, mix all the ingredients for the stir-fry sauce together with 2 tablespoons of water, then set aside.

Heat the cooking oil in a large frying pan or wok on a medium heat. When hot, add the garlic and chillies and cook for 30 seconds.

Stir in the pork, breaking up any large chunks of mince so it cooks evenly, and stir-fry for 5–6 minutes, until well cooked and browned.

Pour the stir-fry sauce into the pan and combine thoroughly. Cook for a further minute, then throw in the basil leaves at the very end just before serving.

Personally, I love this with a crispy fried egg on top with steamed rice. Pickles and egg drop soup also make fine accompaniments.

BONUS

If pork is not your thing, diced chicken thighs will also work great here. For a vegan or vegetarian take, crumble firm tofu into a mince-like texture to turn it into a delicious meat-free meal.

# 15-Minute Express Laksa

● ●
PREP: COOK:
5 MINS 10 MINS

Jetlagged after a flight to Singapore, I sat in a hawker centre and enjoyed a bowl of spicy laksa noodle soup with a friend. In such hot, humid weather, it seemed strange to be slurping a hot broth, but the sweat was worth it.

A good laksa doesn't have to take hours to cook (life doesn't always allow the time to slow-simmer a pot of soup), and my quick version is perfect for a weeknight dinner when you can't be bothered to stand over the stove for longer than needed. Ready in a flash, this laksa tastes like you've made it from scratch.

---

### FOR THE LAKSA

- 100g (3½oz) dried vermicelli rice noodles (thin egg noodles also work here)
- 4-5 raw peeled king prawns (shrimp)
- 2-3 fried tofu puffs
- 2-3 frozen fish balls
- 30g (1oz) beansprouts

### FOR THE SOUP BASE

- 1 tbsp cooking oil of choice
- 1½ tbsp Thai red curry paste
- 1 tbsp medium-hot curry powder
- 200g (7oz) canned full-fat coconut milk
- 500ml (generous 2 cups) chicken or seafood stock
- 1 tbsp fish sauce, plus extra to taste
- ½ tbsp granulated sugar

### TO SERVE

- 1 handful of chopped coriander (cilantro)
- 1-2 lime wedges
- 1 soft-boiled egg

Cook the noodles in a pan of boiling water according to the packet instructions. Drain and rinse briefly under cold running water. Place the noodles in a serving bowl.

Meanwhile, make the soup base. Heat the cooking oil in a deep sauté pan on a medium heat. Add the Thai curry paste and sauté for a minute to release the aroma. Add the curry powder, coconut milk, stock, fish sauce and sugar, then stir until combined. Bring the soup base to a gentle boil, then taste and adjust the seasoning, adding more fish sauce, if needed.

Throw in the prawns, tofu puffs, fish balls and beansprouts. Return the pan to a gentle boil and cook for 2–3 minutes, until the prawns turn pink.

Ladle the soup on top of the noodles in the bowls and scatter over the coriander. Squeeze over the lime, to taste, and serve topped with a soft-boiled egg.

# Hainanese Chicken Rice

● ●
PREP: COOK:
20 MINS 55 MINS

Out of all the recipes in this book, this is the one that I've probably made the most. Without sounding too obvious, the dish originated from the island of Hainan in the most southern part of China, though it is also a well-known across Thailand, Singapore and Malaysia.

The dish is simple but hearty - essentially a whole chicken poached in salted water with ginger and spring onions (green onions), served with rice that is cooked in chicken broth with chicken fat. To be honest, the rice itself is delicious enough to eat on its own, but with the juicy and tender chicken on the side, doused in a soy, chilli (chile) and garlic sauce as well as a ton of fresh coriander (cilantro), it's one of my favourite meals of all time. This isn't just a personal opinion though - it's also a crowd-pleaser. I've made this countless times for friends and there's never any leftovers. After all, anyone who likes chicken will almost certainly love chicken and rice. I wish I'd learned how to make it when I was at uni as it's both budget-friendly and great for prepping ahead.

---

- 6cm (2½in) piece of fresh root ginger, sliced
- 4-5 spring onions (green onions), thickly sliced
- 1 whole chicken, about 1.2-1.5kg (2¾-3lb 3oz), with excess skin and fat trimmed and saved for the rice
- 2 tbsp sea salt

FOR THE RICE
---------------------------------
- 275g (1½ cups) Thai jasmine rice
- 1 tbsp cooking oil of choice (if there is no reserved chicken skin/fat)
- 2cm (¾in) piece of fresh root ginger, sliced

Place the ginger and spring onions in the chicken cavity. Season the chicken generously with the salt, inside and out, and place in a large, deep pot or casserole dish.

Pour in enough water to cover the chicken and bring it to the boil. Once boiling, turn the heat down to a gentle simmer and cook the chicken, covered with the lid, for 35–40 minutes, until it is fully cooked. To test the chicken is ready, pierce the thickest part of the thigh with a skewer to make sure the juices run clear. If the juices are still pink, cook the chicken for another 5 minutes and check again. Carefully remove the cooked chicken from the pot and place it in an ice bath. Let it sit for 5–10 minutes – this will ensure the chicken meat is extra tender and juicy. Reserve the chicken broth in the pot.

Meanwhile, prepare the rice. Wash the rice until the water runs clear. Heat a small frying pan on a high heat and add the reserved trimmed chicken skin and fat to render out for about a minute. If you don't have chicken fat trimmings, use the cooking oil instead.

- 1 spring onion (green onion), cut into 3-4 pieces
- 175ml (¾ cup) chicken broth (from poaching the chicken)
- generous pinch of salt

## FOR THE SPRING ONION SAUCE
----------------------------------

- 2 tbsp light soy sauce
- 1 tsp sesame oil
- 1 tsp rice vinegar
- 1 tbsp minced garlic
- 1 tbsp minced fresh root ginger
- 3 tbsp chicken broth (from poaching the chicken)
- 1 handful of chopped spring onions (green onions)

## FOR THE CHILLI GARLIC SAUCE
----------------------------------

- 1 red chilli (chile), finely chopped
- 2 garlic cloves, minced
- 1 tbsp light soy sauce
- 1 tsp rice vinegar
- pinch of salt
- 100ml (6½ tbsp) chicken broth (from poaching the chicken)

## TO SERVE
----------------------------------

- 1 handful of roughly chopped coriander (cilantro)
- Pickled Cucumber (see p.27)

## PAIRING SUGGESTIONS
----------------------------------

- Lettuce in Oyster & Garlic Sauce (see p.56)
- Chinese Tea Eggs (see p.32)

Next, add the ginger and spring onion to the frying pan and cook for another minute.

Add the rice, chicken broth and the contents of the frying pan (the oil from the chicken will make the rice extra tasty) to a rice cooker. Season with the salt and cook the rice following the instructions on your rice cooker. If cooking conventionally in a pan, follow the method for Steamed Rice (see p.21).

To prepare the sauces, mix the spring onion in one bowl and the chilli and garlic sauce in a separate one. Set both aside for later.

Remove the chicken from the ice bath and drain well. Pull and twist off the chicken legs and wings, and carve around the carcass to remove the breast meat. Chop the chicken into smaller pieces or serve the legs and wings whole with the sliced breast meat.

Divide the rice between serving plates and place the chicken on top. Serve with the sauces for drizzling over, a scattering of coriander, and pickled cucumber on the side. Lettuce in oyster and garlic sauce and Chinese tea eggs make good accompaniments, too.

# Phở Gà

One of the most well-known Vietnamese dishes, if not *the* most, is *phở*. A comforting bowl of this lightly spiced noodle broth was something I enjoyed almost daily, even for breakfast, when I travelled around the country.

This is the sibling to the popular beef *phở*, and is much easier and quicker to make at home - by now, you probably know how much I try to avoid long cooking times whenever I can. It has become almost a ritual for me to use the leftover meat and broth from the Hainanese Chicken Rice (see p.160) to make this - a soothing noodle soup with tender, juicy strips of chicken and lots of fresh coriander (cilantro) and mint. This soup may look unassuming, but the addition of charred onions and ginger, along with the added herbs and spices, turns it into something much more complex and interesting.

---

- 1 brown onion, skin on and halved
- 1 small knob of fresh root ginger
- 1 litre (4⅛ cups) homemade broth from the Hainanese Chicken (see p.160) or ready-made chicken stock
- 2 tsp granulated sugar
- 2 star anise
- 1 Chinese cinnamon stick (cassia)
- 2 tbsp fish sauce
- 1 raw or cooked chicken breast or 2-3 skinless boneless chicken thighs
- 200g (7oz) dried rice stick noodles
- salt and freshly ground black pepper

TO SERVE
- - - - - - - - - - - - - - - - - - - - - - - - - - - - -

- 1 handful each of coriander (cilantro) and mint
- 1 bird's eye chilli (chile), thinly sliced
- lime wedges

To char the onion and ginger, place them on a wire rack over an open flame (I usually do this over my gas hob) and cook for 5–6 minutes, turning halfway with metal tongs, until the outer skin has blackened and charred all over. Remove and set aside.

Pour the broth or stock into a pan and reheat. Add the sugar, star anise, cinnamon stick, fish sauce and charred ginger and onions and bring to a gentle boil. Reduce the heat and simmer for 10 minutes with the lid on, while you prepare everything else. (If cooking the chicken from raw, rather than using ready cooked, poach the breast or thighs in the stock with the rest of the flavourings for 20 minutes, skimming the surface occasionally.)

Meanwhile, cook the noodles according to the packet instructions. Drain and refresh under cold running water and divide the noodles between two serving bowls, then set aside.

Shred the cooked chicken and place on top of the noodles in the serving bowls.

Strain the broth through a fine mesh sieve to remove any solids and season generously with salt and pepper, to taste. Ladle the soup over the rice noodles, scatter with the coriander, mint and chilli and finish with a wedge of lime.

SERVES 2

# Korean Beef Bulgogi

Similar to a Japanese *sukiyaki* or Chinese hot pot, eating at a Korean barbecue restaurant means that you can control how your meal is cooked – there's a stove-top barbecue or griddle right at the table! If you've had the pleasure of experiencing a delicious Korean barbecue, you'll also know the myriad meats and sides you can choose from. One of my favourites is beef bulgogi. "Bulgogi" literally means "fire meat" and it's typically thinly sliced beef (or pork) marinated in a sweet and spicy sauce. When barbecued, it takes on a chargrilled flavour and is best enjoyed as a filling in a Korean *ssam* (or lettuce wrap to you and me). I devoured tons of this dish during my travels in Seoul in the summer of 2016, when I learned the best way to make the perfect *ssam*.

---

- 500g (1lb 2oz) ribeye or sirloin beef steak, cut into 1cm (½in) thick slices (this also works great with pork shoulder)
- 2 tbsp cooking oil of choice
- 1 brown onion, thinly sliced
- 1 handful of chopped spring onions (green onions)

## FOR THE MARINADE
------------------------------------
- 1 garlic clove, minced
- 1 thumb-sized piece of fresh root ginger, peeled and minced
- 1 tbsp gochujang paste
- 1 tbsp gochugaru, Korean chilli (chile) flakes, (optional)
- ½ tbsp mirin (optional)
- 1 tbsp light soy sauce
- 1 tbsp runny honey

## TO SERVE
------------------------------------
- 8-10 butterhead lettuce leaves, optional
- 50g (1¾oz) kimchi, sliced
- Steamed Rice (see p.21), optional

## PAIRING SUGGESTIONS
------------------------------------
- Japchae (see p.98)
- Kimchi Tofu Stew (see p.94)

To make the steak easier to slice, you can freeze it for 2 hours until firm prior to cooking – you don't want it frozen solid, but freezing the meat makes it much easier to slice thinly.

Mix together all the ingredients for the marinade in a shallow dish. Add the beef slices and mix thoroughly until the meat is well coated in the marinade. Cover and leave to marinate in the refrigerator for at least 1 hour, preferably overnight.

When you're ready to cook, heat the oil in a large frying pan or wok on a medium–high heat. Once hot, add the onion and sauté for a few minutes until translucent and softened.

Add the marinated beef to the pan or wok with any remaining marinade and cook for about 15 minutes. Refrain from moving the meat around too much to allow it to brown slightly. (For a more chargrilled flavour, cook the beef in batches in a griddle pan.) Toss in the spring onions towards the end and give everything one last stir before transferring to a serving bowl.

To make a *ssam*, place a few slices of the beef in a lettuce leaf wrap and top with a slice or two of kimchi. You can also serve the beef with a bowl of rice, if liked.

BONUS

Like many dishes that call for marinating, the longer you do so the better the flavour. This is definitely a recipe that is worth getting organized for.

# Set Menu

→ CHAR SIU (BBQ PORK) — (152)
→ SPICY THAI BASIL PORK — (156)
→ HAINANESE CHICKEN RICE — (160)
→ PHỞ GÀ — (162)

# Sharing the

# Love

# Sharing the Love

Growing up, the way I was shown love through cooking is so ingrained that making others happy with delicious plates of food has since become second nature to me.

I firmly believe that if cooking and feeding others is the language of love, then it is mine. Growing up, the way I was shown love through cooking is so ingrained that making others happy with delicious plates of food has since become second nature to me. I'll be the first to admit that I've always offered to cook for my boyfriends, even those I dated for a short period of time. Don't they say, the way to a man's heart is through his stomach? I know it surely is the way to mine.

Now that I live alone and have my own space, I love to host friends for dinner as well as organize a few potluck parties throughout the year. A potluck party is my favourite kind of gathering, because everyone brings a dish, so there's a huge selection of food on the table – and it's all made with love. It doesn't get more wholesome than that.

In this chapter, you'll find many recipes that would be perfect for a potluck party. If you're looking for a quick and easy dish to bring to a dinner party, the moreish Son-in-Law Eggs (see p.176) is perfect. The eggs are sweet, savoury and spicy all at the same time and a real crowd-pleaser, for sure. The Teriyaki Chicken Skewers (see p.182) are great for barbecues and can be made ahead of time, so super convenient. Let's also not forget how everyone loves a dessert at a gathering, and the one that always goes down well is my favourite cheesecake of all time, the Matcha Burnt Basque Cheesecake (see p.208).

That said, the stars of the show in this chapter are the dumplings, wontons and baos. They are my answer to that timeless question: "If you could only eat one thing, what would it be?". Okay, I know

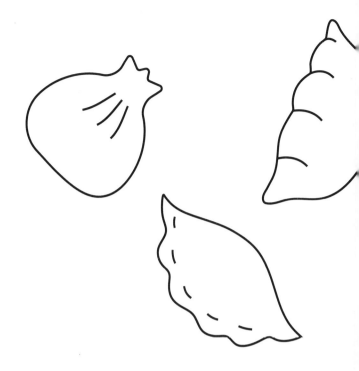

they are three different types of food, but it's impossible to choose between them.

During the 2020 pandemic, aside from experimenting with different dishes in the kitchen, I spent a lot of time perfecting my dumpling-making skills. Before then, I'd never really fully grasped the entire process as I'd always had my mum or grandma on hand to help. With the inevitable need to isolate, and no grandma to assist, it left me to tackle the one step that I'd always tried to avoid – rolling out the dumpling wrappers. In the past, I'd shied away from this step in the dumpling-making process. The prospect of rolling out each dumpling wrapper, one at a time, had always seemed a bit tedious and dull. But in time, when I finally got the hang of it after many practice goes, the rolling process became really therapeutic. Before I knew it, I was making dumplings on a regular basis – putting a television show on in the background, rolling the dough out, one piece at a time, then proceeding to pleat each dumpling by hand. It really was a labour of love. I became obsessed, regularly posting my creations on social media, and my followers loved to see them too. Feeling majorly encouraged by this, I even tempted my usually fussy housemates to try some.

Once things started to open up again after the pandemic, I started hosting dumpling-making parties at home. My friends would come round, we'd catch up over making the dough, then I would show them how to pleat, and we'd laugh or applaud at how successful the dumplings turned out to be. It's definitely a lot more fun, and they're quicker to make, when others are by your side. If you enjoy eating dumplings, I really would suggest you try making them too. It's good fun, I promise!

# Chinese Spring Onion Pancakes

● ●
PREP: COOK:
20 MINS* 1 HOUR

*plus resting

Fragrant and totally moreish, these savoury pancakes are vegan and come with a tangy dipping sauce. They are made with a dough, rather than a batter, and filled with an aromatic mixture of spring onions (green onions), sesame oil and Chinese five-spice.

I always make a big batch of pancakes, so I have leftovers to freeze and enjoy another day as a snack or accompaniment to a larger meal. To freeze, place a small piece of baking (parchment) paper on a baking tray (sheet), top with a rolled-out pancake and a second piece of baking paper. Repeat until all the dough has been used and the pancakes are layered, with a sheet of paper in between. Freeze until firm, then transfer to a ziplock bag. When ready to serve, cook the pancakes from frozen, following the instructions in the method.

---

## FOR THE DOUGH

- 400g (3 cups) plain (all-purpose) flour, plus extra for dusting
- 200ml (scant 1 cup) lukewarm water

## FOR THE FILLING

- 150ml (⅔ cup) vegetable oil, plus extra for frying pancakes
- 100g (3½oz) spring onions (green onions), finely chopped
- 60g (scant ½ cup) plain (all-purpose) flour
- 1 tsp salt
- 1 tbsp sesame oil
- 1 tbsp Chinese five-spice powder

To make the dough, tip the flour into a large mixing bowl. Gradually pour in the lukewarm water, mixing with a wooden spoon until a ragged dough. Knead the dough on a lightly floured work surface for 30 seconds, until it forms a rough ball shape.

Wrap the dough in cling film (plastic wrap) and leave to rest for 30 minutes (leaving it to rest makes the kneading process much easier, my grandma used to say). The science behind it is that the flour gradually hydrates after adding the water and becomes softer to work with during resting. Most of the hard work is done during this time and there's no need to continuously work the dough.

Meanwhile, prepare the filling. In a small pan, heat the vegetable oil until gently smoking. Put the spring onions in a heatproof bowl and pour the hot oil over – the oil will sizzle and cook the spring onions. Add the flour, salt, sesame oil and Chinese five-spice powder. Mix to combine and adjust the seasoning with more salt, if needed. Set aside the paste to cool.

Make the dipping sauce by mixing all the ingredients together in a bowl. Set aside until ready to use.

After the dough has rested, knead for a few minutes until smooth and form into a ball shape. Divide the dough into 8 equal pieces.

## FOR THE DIPPING SAUCE

-----------------------------------

- 1 tbsp light soy sauce
- 1 tsp sesame oil
- 1 tsp rice vinegar or
  apple cider vinegar

## PAIRING SUGGESTIONS

-----------------------------------

- Chinese Five-Spice Chicken
  (see p.130)
- Spiced Lamb Soup Noodles
  (see p.148)

Using a rolling pin, roll out one piece of dough on a lightly floured work surface into a large, thin round pancake, about 20cm (8in) in diameter. Cover the rest of the dough portions with cling film (plastic wrap) while you work. Spread about 2 tablespoons of the filling evenly over the pancake, leaving a 2.5cm (1in) border around the edge. Roll the pancake tightly into a log shape. Next, roll the log to form a swirl, similar to a Danish. Set aside while you repeat this process with the other pieces of dough.

Once all the dough swirls are made, take one and flatten it slightly in the palm of your hand. Then, using a rolling pin, roll it out into a flat pancake, about 1cm (½in) thick. Repeat with the rest of the dough.

To cook the pancakes, heat 1 tablespoon of cooking oil in a large frying pan on a high heat. (You could have two pans on the go at the same time, if feasible.) Once hot, carefully lower a pancake into the pan and cook for 2–3 minutes on each side. Check that it's golden brown before you flip it over. You may need to reduce the heat to medium once the pancake is turned over to prevent it burning – it should take no more than 4–6 minutes per pancake. Remove from the pan and place on kitchen paper to remove any excess oil. Eat straightaway or keep warm in a low oven while you cook the remaining pancakes.

Serve the pancakes whole or cut into strips and enjoy warm with the dipping sauce by the side.

**FUN FACT**

The Chinese translation for spring onion (green onion) is "onion" (*cong*). The translation for brown onion is "foreign onion" (*yang cong*) as they were imported at a later date.

# Classic
# Spring Rolls

春卷

Who doesn't love a freshly made spring roll? No, seriously. I don't think I've ever had someone turn down one of these. The warm, crisp golden pastry encasing a seasoned vegetable filling is unmatched - I can eat several in one go, even without a dipping sauce.

Feel free to make this recipe your own by including some cooked minced (ground) pork, steamed and shredded chicken or crumbled firm tofu for added protein.

---

- 20 small pre-made spring roll wrappers, plus extra if you need to double wrap to prevent leakage
- 250ml (1 cup plus 1 tbsp) cooking oil of choice, for frying
- sweet chilli sauce, to serve

## FOR THE FILLING

- 50g (1¾oz) dried wood ear mushrooms
- 4-5 fresh or dried shiitake mushrooms, finely sliced
- 1 tbsp cooking oil of choice
- 4 garlic cloves, minced
- 1 tbsp finely grated fresh root ginger
- 2 mild red chillies (chiles), finely chopped
- 250g (9oz) sweetheart cabbage, finely shredded
- 50g (1¾oz) beansprouts
- 2 small carrots, coarsely grated
- 1 tsp sesame oil
- 1 tbsp light soy sauce
- pinch of granulated sugar
- pinch of MSG, optional
- salt, to taste

## FOR THE DIPPING SAUCE

- 1 tbsp light soy sauce
- 1 tsp sesame oil
- 1 tsp rice vinegar or apple cider vinegar

To start to make the filling, rehydrate the wood ear mushrooms. Put them in a heatproof bowl and pour over enough just-boiled water from a kettle to cover. In a separate bowl, do the same with the dried shiitake, if using. Leave to soak for 10 minutes, until rehydrated, then drain well and thinly slice.

To continue to make the filling, heat the cooking oil in a large frying pan on a medium heat. Add the garlic, ginger and chillies and cook for a minute until fragrant. Add the mushrooms and prepared vegetables and stir-fry for 3–4 minutes, until softened and wilted. Add all the filling seasoning ingredients to the pan. Mix until combined and adjust the seasoning, adding more salt, if needed. Spoon the filling into a bowl and allow to cool completely.

Meanwhile, mix all the ingredients for the dipping sauce in a bowl and set aside for later.

Separate the spring roll wrappers by carefully peeling them apart. Place them on a work surface or plate ready for use. Prepare a small bowl of water and set to one side.

To assemble the spring rolls, set a wrapper diagonally in front of you. Place 1 tablespoon of the filling in the corner closest to you, leaving a 1cm (½in) border around the edge. Roll the corner of the wrapper closest to you over the filling, then fold in the corners on each side onto the filling to create a cylindrical shape. Then, gently pressing each end to keep the shape, roll it away from you into a spring roll.

To seal the spring roll, dip a finger in the bowl of water and wet the top corner of the wrapper, then fold it over and press to seal. Repeat to make 20 small spring rolls.

To cook the spring rolls, heat the cooking oil in a small pan on a medium–high heat until hot, about 160–170°C (320–338°F). Add the spring rolls in batches and fry for 3–5 minutes, until golden brown and crisp. (You can also do this in a deep-fat fryer, if you have one.) Drain briefly on kitchen paper to remove any excess oil, while you cook the rest.

Serve the spring rolls hot with bowls of the dipping sauce and sweet chilli sauce on the side.

# Son-in-Law Eggs

● PREP: 5 MINS    ● COOK: 25 MINS

Legend has it that the name of this popular Thai snack came from a concerned and protective mother, who after finding out that her daughter wasn't being treated well by her son-in-law, fried up two boiled eggs as a warning to him!

Whether or not the story is true, the combination of soft-centred yolk with crisp egg white, not to mention the sweet, tangy sauce, and topping of crispy shallots and fresh coriander (cilantro) is out of this world. Hands up, the first time I tried this dish, I ate four eggs in 5 minutes as they were so mind-blowingly delicious - the flavour and texture encapsulates perfectly everything Thai food has to offer in just one bite. They're addictive, and I challenge you to eat just one!

---

- 10 eggs, at room temperature
- 1 tbsp white vinegar
- 2 tbsp cooking oil of choice
- 1 shallot, thinly sliced
- 1 tsp dried chilli flakes (crushed red pepper flakes)
- 1 handful of fresh coriander (cilantro)

FOR THE SAUCE
- - - - - - - - - - - - - - - - - - -
- 2-3 tbsp tamarind paste
- 3 tbsp light soft brown sugar
- 2 tbsp fish sauce

PAIRING SUGGESTIONS
- - - - - - - - - - - - - - - - - - -
- Spicy Thai Basil Pork (see p.156)

Bring a pan of water to the boil and add the vinegar. Gently lower in the eggs and boil for 7 minutes for a runny centre, or cook for 1 minute longer if you prefer a firmer yolk.

While the eggs are cooking, heat the cooking oil in a small frying pan on a medium heat. Add the shallot and fry until golden. Remove and drain on kitchen paper, saving the shallot oil in the pan.

Place the cooked eggs in a bowl of iced water for 5 minutes to stop them cooking any further. Carefully peel the eggs and pat dry with kitchen paper to remove any water or moisture as otherwise they will splatter in the hot oil, then set aside.

Heat the pan with the shallot oil and fry the boiled eggs, turning occasionally, for 4–5 minutes, until the outside is golden and wrinkly. Remove with a slotted spoon and place on a serving plate.

Using the same pan containing the shallot oil, add all the ingredients for the sauce with 2 tablespoons of water and stir until combined. Bring the sauce to a gentle bubble and cook until thickened slightly. It should take about 4–5 minutes. If it's a little dry, add an extra splash of water. Taste test to see if the sauce needs any adjusting in terms of sourness or sweetness.

To assemble, cut the eggs in half, then drizzle the tamarind sauce over and garnish with crispy shallots, chilli flakes and coriander. Serve with spicy Thai basil pork for a larger meal.

# Taiwanese Fried Chicken

台 式 咸 酥 鸡

**PREP:** 20 MINS*

**COOK:** 15 MINS

*plus marinating

Everybody loves fried chicken, right - especially when it's crispy and crunchy on the outside, and super juicy and tender in the middle.

My love of fried chicken was reinforced by a visit to the street-food night markets of Taiwan. They're a must if you ever visit the country as you'll discover all sorts of tantalizing food stalls, especially those selling crispy fried chicken. I made sure I sampled all the best they had to offer on my visit, and I still dream about them to this day. The golden, bite-sized pieces of chicken make the perfect on-the-go snack.

This is my super-easy version of Taiwanese fried chicken: simply chop, marinade and deep fry. I've also provided two alternative ways to cook the chicken, including air-fried and oven-baked, but whichever method you choose will result in moist, tender nuggets with a crisp coating. Personally, chicken thigh is my favourite cut when it comes to fried chicken as it remains moist, but you can definitely substitute it for chicken breast, if you prefer (see my Bonus tip).

Just remember, it's a dangerous game, crispy fried chicken is so addictive that before you know it you'll be dreaming about it, just like me.

---

- 700g (1lb 8oz) skinless boneless chicken thigh fillets, cut into bite-sized pieces
- about 300ml (1¼ cups) cooking oil of choice
- 15g (½oz) basil leaves

**FOR THE MARINADE**

- 1 tbsp cornflour (cornstarch)
- 1 tsp Chinese five-spice powder
- 1 tsp ground white pepper
- 1 tsp garlic powder

Mix all the ingredients for the marinade together in a shallow dish to make a loose paste. Add the chicken thigh pieces and spoon the marinade all over, turning the chicken until evenly coated. Cover and leave to marinate in the fridge for 30 minutes.

Just before you are ready to cook, combine all the coating ingredients together in a shallow dish. Add the chicken and turn until evenly coated, then pat off any excess.

In a saucepan or deep-fat fryer, heat about 300ml (1¼ cups) of cooking oil (depending on the size of the pan) to 180°C/356°F.

Carefully, add a third of the chicken thigh pieces to the pan and deep-fry for 2 minutes. Remove with a slotted spoon and place on a kitchen paper-lined plate while you cook the rest of the chicken in two batches. Drain all the cooked chicken on kitchen paper.

- 1 tsp paprika powder
- 1 tsp dried chilli flakes
  (crushed red pepper flakes)
- ½ tsp salt
- 1 tsp granulated sugar
- 2 tbsp light soy sauce
- ½ tbsp Chinese cooking wine
- 1 garlic clove, minced
- 1 tbsp cooking oil of choice

## FOR THE COATING
------------------------------------
- 2 tbsp cornflour
  (cornstarch)
- 70g (½ cup) tapioca or
  potato flour
- 1 tsp baking powder

## FOR THE SEASONING
------------------------------------
- ½ tsp salt
- ½ tsp chilli powder
- ½ tsp garlic powder
- ½ tsp ground black pepper
- ½ tsp Chinese five-spice
  powder

## PAIRING SUGGESTIONS
------------------------------------
- Pickled Cucumber (see p.27)
  or Carrot & Daikon Pickle
  (see p.28)
- Shanghai Spring Onion Oil
  Noodles (see p.42)
- Kimchi Fried Rice
  (see p.116)

Reheat the oil to 180°C/356°F, if needed. Fry the chicken thigh pieces for a second time in batches for 2 minutes, until golden brown and crispy. Once cooked, remove and place the chicken on a wire rack to drain off any excess oil.

Strain the oil to remove any solids or crumbs, then return it to the pan or fryer and reheat to 180°C/356°F. Fry the basil leaves in batches for 10–15 seconds, until they turn a dark green colour, taking care that they don't burn. Remove with a slotted spoon and drain on kitchen paper to remove any excess oil.

To serve, mix all the ingredients for the seasoning together and sprinkle it over the hot chicken, then scatter the fried basil leaves on top. For a refreshing side, pair the chicken with pickled cucumber and/or carrot and daikon pickle. The Shanghai spring onion oil noodles and kimchi fried rice go particularly well with the chicken, too.

Instead of deep frying the chicken, you may wish to try these alternative cooking methods.

**TO AIR FRY** Spray your air-fryer basket with cooking oil, then drizzle a little extra oil over each piece of prepared chicken thigh Cook the chicken at 200°C/400°F for about 15 minutes, turning it and brushing with more oil at 5-minute intervals. If the chicken pieces are thick or big, they may need an extra 2–3 minutes to cook through. Remove and place on a wire rack. Serve as above.

**TO OVEN BAKE** Preheat the oven to 200°C/180°C fan/400°F/Gas 6. Drizzle a little oil over each piece of prepared chicken thigh. Place on a wire rack over a roasting tin. Cook the chicken for around 20 minutes, turning halfway and drizzling over more oil, if needed, until golden brown and cooked through. Once cooked, serve as above.

BONUS

To use chicken breasts instead of thighs, butterfly 2 chicken breasts to make two large, flat pieces (or several smaller ones, if preferred). To do this, put one of the chicken breasts on a preparation board and, with your hand flat on top of it, use a sharp knife to slice into one side of the breast, starting at the thicker end and finishing at the thinnest point - be careful not to cut it all the way through. Open out the butterflied chicken breast, then bash with the end of a rolling pin until an even thickness, about 1cm (½in). Repeat with the second chicken breast before spreading with the marinade paste and crumb coating.

# Teriyaki Chicken Skewers

● ●
PREP:    COOK:
20 MINS*  15 MINS

*plus marinating

If you've ever travelled to Japan, you'll no doubt have come across teriyaki - grilled or barbecued food in a sweet, sticky glaze. These Japanese-inspired chicken skewers, marinated in a delicious umami-packed teriyaki sauce, are a real crowd-pleaser, particularly with kids, My little brothers love them as they are sweet in flavour and the chicken becomes tender and juicy when cooked.

I've used the velveting technique here (see p.128); adding bicarbonate of soda (baking soda) and cornflour (cornstarch) to tenderize the meat while marinating.

---

- 1kg (2lb 2oz) skinless boneless chicken thigh fillets, cut into bite-sized pieces
- 2 tbsp light soy sauce
- 1 tbsp runny honey
- ½ tsp toasted sesame seeds
- 1 handful of chopped spring onions (green onions)

FOR THE MARINADE
------------------------------------
- 1 tbsp cornflour (cornstarch)
- ½ tsp bicarbonate of soda (baking soda)
- 2 tbsp light soy sauce
- 3 tbsp soft light brown sugar or runny honey
- 1 tbsp mirin
- 3 garlic cloves, minced
- ½ tbsp finely grated fresh root ginger
- pinch of salt

PAIRING SUGGESTIONS
------------------------------------
- your choice of dumplings (see pp.184-197)
- Chinese Spring Onion Pancakes (see p.172)
- Classic Spring Rolls (see p.174)

Mix all the ingredients for the marinade together in a bowl. Add the chicken and mix thoroughly to ensure each piece is coated. Cover and leave to marinate for about 15 minutes in the fridge.

Meanwhile, soak 10 bamboo skewers in water to prevent them burning during cooking.

When ready, thread the marinated chicken pieces onto the skewers, about 5–6 pieces on each, depending on size.

Preheat the grill (broiler) to high. Place the chicken skewers on a foil-lined baking tray (sheet) under the grill and cook for 12 minutes, until cooked through. Turn the skewers halfway through grilling and baste with any leftover marinade. (You can also cook the skewers on a barbecue.)

While the skewers are cooking, mix together the soy sauce and honey to make a glaze.

Brush the glaze all over the cooked chicken and return the skewers to the grill for another 2 minutes, until glossy and golden.

Scatter the toasted sesame seeds and spring onions over the chicken skewers. Serve with dumplings, spring onion pancakes and spring rolls for a great dinner party!

# Dumplings, Baos & Wontons

I love dumplings. If I had to choose one type of food to eat for the rest of my life, I would probably go for dumplings – they just never get boring. Dumplings are so versatile that you can select the fillings to suit whatever your heart desires. Veggie? No problem. Vegan? Absolutely. Meat lover? Most certainly…

On the next few pages, we are going to dive deep into my favourite dumplings, baos and wontons. They come in different shapes and sizes, tastes and textures, and can be cooked in a variety of ways, whether that be steamed, boiled, pan-fried or deep-fried. Let's begin…

# Chicken Potstickers

Known as gyoza in Japan, these pan-fried dumplings are called potstickers in China because of the way they stick to the pan, giving them their signature crispy, golden bottom. That said, if you'd rather steam or boil the dumplings, that's also fine - they'll still be delicious, but they just won't be potstickers. Technically, these potstickers can be filled with anything you like, such as pork and leek (see p.190), but personally, I love this juicy chicken filling.

This recipe makes plenty of dumplings, so don't feel you have to cook them all in one sitting. I often freeze a batch, and they make a great speedy meal when I'm short on time. To do this, place the uncooked dumplings, spaced out evenly, on a baking tray (sheet) lined with baking (parchment) paper. Place the tray in the freezer until the dumplings are frozen solid. Once frozen, remove and place them in a ziplock freezer bag. Do not put the dumplings in the ziplock bag when fresh as they will stick together during freezing. The potstickers can be cooked directly from frozen, just follow the method below.

---

- 2-3 tbsp cooking oil of choice
- 1 handful of finely chopped spring onions (green onions)
- 1 tsp black sesame seeds
- The Ultimate Dumpling Sauce (see p.26), to serve

## FOR THE DOUGH

- 250g (scant 2 cups) plain (all-purpose) flour, plus extra for dusting
- pinch of salt
- 150ml (⅔ cup) lukewarm water

**MAKING THE DOUGH** Tip the flour and salt into a large mixing bowl. Gradually pour in the water, mixing with a wooden spoon to make a ragged dough. Knead the dough on a lightly floured work surface for 30 seconds, until it comes together into a rough ball.

Wrap the dough in cling film (plastic wrap) and leave to rest for 30 minutes (leaving it to rest makes the kneading process much easier, my grandma used to say). The science behind it is that the flour gradually hydrates after adding the water and becomes softer to work with during resting. Most of the hard work is done during this time and there's no need to continuously work the dough. After resting, briefly knead the dough again until a smooth ball.

**MAKING THE FILLING** In a separate mixing bowl, combine the cabbage with the salt. Allow to stand for 10 minutes, or until some of the water in the cabbage is released. Give the cabbage a quick squeeze to remove any excess water, then drain.

Return the cabbage to the mixing bowl and add the rest of the chicken filling ingredients.

## FOR THE CHICKEN FILLING

- 200g (7oz) Chinese or napa cabbage, shredded
- ½ tsp salt
- 250g (9oz) skinless boneless chicken thighs, finely minced/ground (substitute with minced/ground turkey for a leaner option)
- 4-5 shiitake mushrooms, finely diced
- 2 spring onions (green onions), finely chopped
- 3-4 garlic cloves, minced
- 2 tbsp light soy sauce
- ½ tsp ground white pepper
- 1 egg

Stir the filling continuously with a fork in one direction for 4 minutes, until combined. Stirring in one direction helps the protein strands to bind together more quickly. If you want to taste test it at this point, fry a spoonful of the mixture until cooked through and adjust the seasoning, if needed.

**SHAPING THE WRAPPERS** Once the dough is ready, pierce a hole all the way through the centre of the dough with your thumb and begin to stretch out the hole until it forms a large ring doughnut shape. Make a cut in the "doughnut" with a knife to open it out into a log. Roll the log out until the same circumference as your forefinger at its fattest point, then divide it into quarters. Cut one of the quarters into 8–10 pieces. Repeat with the three remaining pieces of dough. Cover with a damp tea (dish) towel or cling film (plastic wrap) to prevent the pieces drying out.

Take one piece of dough and roll it into a ball. Place on a lightly floured chopping board or work surface and press it flat, then roll it out to the size of your palm. For best results, roll the edges out slightly thinner than the middle, as this will make the dumplings easier to pleat. Repeat with the rest of the dough portions.

**FILLING AND PLEATING** Place the rolled-out wrapper in the middle of the palm of your non-dominant hand, spoon 1 tablespoon of the filling into the middle. If a beginner, leave a 2.5cm (1in) border around the edge of the dough to allow for pleating. (More experienced dumpling makers can leave a narrower border!)

To pleat the dumplings, fold the wrapper in half, pinch the edges together in the middle. Working on the left side first, pleat the wrapper using your thumb and forefinger, sealing the edges together as you go, then move to the other side and repeat. Don't worry if the first few dumplings don't look good – practice makes perfect! As long as they are sealed with no holes, they're good to go.

Repeat until all the wrappers are filled and pleated. You may want to cover the filled dumplings to prevent them drying out.

**COOKING** Heat 1 tablespoon of the cooking oil in a large frying pan (with a lid) on a medium heat. Before the oil is too hot, arrange the dumplings slightly spaced out in the pan and cook in batches for 3–4 minutes, or until the bottoms are golden brown and crisp. Add a good splash of water to the pan, cover with the lid and let the dumplings steam for 4–5 minutes, until the liquid is absorbed and the filling cooked through. Remove from the pan, then cook the second batch, adding another 1 tablespoon of oil. Cook a third batch of the dumplings in the same way, if needed.

Once all the dumplings are cooked, place them on a serving plate and scatter the spring onions and sesame seeds over. Enjoy with the dumpling sauce on the side.

Instead of pan-frying the dumplings, you may wish to try the alternative cooking methods, opposite.

**TO BOIL** Bring a large pan of water to the boil and add the dumplings. (You may have to cook them in batches, depending on how many you're cooking and how big the pan is.) Bring the water back to a gentle boil and cook for 5 minutes, until the dumplings float to the surface. Remove with a slotted spoon, drain and place on a serving dish. Serve with soy sauce and a dash of Chinese black vinegar.

**TO STEAM** Bring a large pan of water to the boil. Line a bamboo or metal steamer basket with baking (parchment) paper. Next, place the dumplings, spaced out so they aren't touching, in the lined steamer. (You may have to steam them in batches, depending on how many you're cooking and how big the steamer is.) Cover and steam for 5 minutes, until cooked through. Remove the cooked dumplings with tongs. Serve with soy sauce and a dash of Chinese black vinegar.

**TO DEEP-FRY** Pour enough cooking oil into a small pan until about 5–7.5cm (2–3in) deep. Heat the oil on a medium–high heat until it reaches 160–170°C (320–338°F). Add the dumplings (in batches) and fry for 4–5 minutes, until crispy and cooked through. (You can also do this in a deep-fat fryer.) Drain briefly on kitchen paper. Serve with sweet chilli sauce or my Ultimate Dumpling Sauce (see p.26).

# Pork & Leek Sheng Jīan Baos

猪肉生煎包

●       ●
PREP:    COOK:
1 HOUR*  30 MINS

*plus proving

This is the classic Shanghai pan-fried bao with crispy bottom and fluffy top - my (and my family's) all-time favourite when growing up in the city. I prefer this juicy pork and fragrant leek filling over most others and like to serve the buns with a generous amount of Chinese black vinegar and chilli (chile) oil drizzled over. The dough is half-yeasted, meaning the buns puff up a little when cooked. They are different to the bao buns you may be familiar with, which are fully yeasted and very fluffy with a springy texture when steamed.

---

- 2-3 tbsp cooking oil of choice, for frying
- 1 large handful of finely chopped spring onions (green onions)
- 2 tsp black sesame seeds
- The Ultimate Dumpling Sauce (see p.26), to serve

### FOR THE DOUGH
--------------------------------

- 250g (scant 2 cups) plain (all-purpose) flour, plus extra for dusting
- 1 tsp instant dried yeast
- 1 tsp granulated sugar
- 150ml (⅔ cup) lukewarm water

### FOR THE PORK FILLING
--------------------------------

- 250g (9oz) minced (ground) pork
- 75g (2½oz) leek, finely chopped
- 1 egg
- 2 tbsp light soy sauce
- ½ tsp ground white pepper
- 1 tsp sesame oil
- ¼ tsp salt

**MAKING THE DOUGH** Combine the flour with the yeast and sugar in a large mixing bowl. Gradually pour in the water, mixing with a wooden spoon to make a ragged dough. Knead on a lightly floured surface for a minute until it comes together into a rough ball. Return the dough to the bowl and cover with a damp tea (dish) towel or cling film (plastic wrap). Leave the dough to rise in a warm place until doubled in size, about 1–2 hours depending on the room temperature.

**MAKING THE FILLING** Meanwhile, in a mixing bowl, mix all the ingredients for the filling, stirring continuously with a fork in one direction for 4 minutes, until combined. Stirring in one direction helps the protein strands to bind together more quickly. If you want to taste test at this point, fry a spoonful of the mixture until cooked through and adjust the seasoning, if needed.

**SHAPING THE WRAPPERS** Once the dough has risen, punch out the air and knead several times on a lightly floured work surface until a smoothish ball of dough. Pierce a hole all the way through the centre of the dough with your thumb and begin to stretch out the hole until it forms a large ring doughnut shape. Make a cut in the "doughnut" with a knife to open it out into a log. Roll the log out until the same circumference as your forefinger at its fattest point, then divide it into 20 pieces. Cover the dough pieces with a damp tea towel or cling film to prevent them drying out.

Take one piece of dough and roll it into a ball. Place on a lightly floured chopping board or work surface and press it flat, then roll out to the size of your palm. For best results, roll the edges out slightly thinner than the middle, as this will make the dumplings easier to pleat. Repeat with the rest of the dough portions.

**FILLING AND PLEATING** Place the rolled-out wrapper in the middle of the palm of your non-dominant hand, spoon 1 tablespoon of the filling into the middle. If a beginner, leave a 2.5cm (1in) border around the edge of the dough to allow for pleating. (More experienced dumpling makers can leave a narrower border!)

To pleat the baos, support the wrapper with filling in your non-dominant hand, and use your dominant hand to pleat the dough. Working in a circular motion, pleat your way around the bao, sealing the edges together as you go (see p.192). Don't worry if the first few baos don't look good – practice makes perfect! As long as they are sealed with no holes, they're good to go.

Repeat until all the wrappers are filled and pleated. Cover the filled and shaped baos as you work through the rest to prevent them drying out – they may rise a little since the dough is yeasted.

**COOKING** Heat 1 tablespoon of the cooking oil in a large frying pan (with a lid) on a medium heat. Before the oil is too hot, arrange the baos slightly spaced out in the pan and cook in batches for 7 minutes, or until the bottoms are golden brown and crisp. Pour enough water into the pan, so it's 1cm (½in) deep. Cover with the lid and let the baos steam for 4–5 minutes, until the liquid is absorbed and the filling cooked through. Remove from the pan, then cook the second batch, adding another 1 tablespoon of oil. Cook a third batch of the baos in the same way, if needed.

Once all the baos are cooked, place them on a serving plate and scatter the spring onions and sesame seeds over. Enjoy with the dumpling sauce on the side.

SERVES 4
(MAKES 20)

# Cumin Lamb
# Steamed Baos

羊肉包子

PREP:     COOK:
1 HOUR*   40 MINS

*plus proving

My stepdad is from the city of Xi'an in Shaanxi Province, central China. Home to a large Muslim community, halal influences shape the cooking there, so dishes using lamb and mutton are a common sight in street-food markets. One of my stepdad's favourite things to eat is a lamb skewer (羊肉串儿), which is typically seasoned with cumin and chilli (chile), then grilled over a flame. The aroma is fantastic, and it's almost impossible not to buy a few for a delicious road-side snack.

With this in mind, I've experimented with the delicious combination of tender lamb and spices as a filling for a beloved bao. The first time I made these buns, biting into the juicy, fragrant filling inside the fluffy steamed bao was so good, I immediately went for a second, then a third, so, I hope you'll enjoy them too.

---

- 1 large handful of finely chopped spring onions (green onions), optional
- 2 tsp black sesame seeds, optional
- The Ultimate Dumpling Sauce (see p.26), to serve

### FOR THE DOUGH
- - - - - - - - - - - - - - - - - - - - - - - - - - - - - - - -

- 250g (scant 2 cups) plain (all-purpose) flour, plus extra for dusting
- 1 tsp instant dried yeast
- 1 tsp granulated sugar
- 150ml (⅔ cup) lukewarm water

### FOR THE LAMB FILLING
- - - - - - - - - - - - - - - - - - - - - - - - - - - - - - - -

- 250g (9oz) minced (ground) lamb, preferably 20% fat
- 50g (1¾oz) leek, finely chopped
- 50g (1¾oz) carrot, grated
- 1 egg
- 2 tbsp light soy sauce
- 2 tsp ground cumin
- 2 tsp Chinese cooking wine
- ½ tsp ground white pepper
- 1 tsp minced garlic
- 1 red chilli (chile), finely chopped
- ½ tsp salt
- ½ tsp MSG, optional

**MAKING THE DOUGH, FILLING, AND SHAPING THE WRAPPERS** Prepare the dough, make the lamb filling, then roll out and shape the dough wrappers ready for filling, following the instructions for the Pork & Leek Sheng Jian Baos on page 190.

**FILLING AND PLEATING** Place the rolled-out wrapper in the middle of the palm of your non-dominant hand, spoon 1 tablespoon of the filling into the middle. If a beginner, leave a 2.5cm (1in) border around the edge of the dough to allow for pleating. (More experienced dumpling makers can leave a narrower border!)

To pleat the baos, follow the instructions for the Pork & Leek Sheng Jian Baos on page 191. If you prefer to skip the pleating completely, just pinch the edges of the dough together to ensure there are no holes. Flip the baos upside down so the smooth side is on top and you're good to go. Cover and leave to prove for another 15–20 minutes.

**COOKING** Prepare a large pan and a bamboo steamer basket lined with steamer paper. You could use baking (parchment) paper with 7–8 holes cut out to let steam through. Place a small heatproof bowl upside down in the pan, pour in enough water to come halfway up the sides of the bowl and bring to the boil. Place the steamer basket on top of the bowl in the pan and steam the baos in batches for 15 minutes. Switch off the heat and leave the baos in the steamer with the lid on for a further 5 minutes.

Remove and cook the rest of the baos in batches, replenishing the water when needed. (You may want to enjoy the fresh batch as you wait for the second batch to cook as they are best eaten when piping hot.)

Enjoy with the dumpling sauce by the side. If liked, scatter the spring onions and sesame seeds over the baos before serving.

# Vegan Sheng Jian Baos

纯素生煎包

Now you've seen my recipes for Pork & Leek (see p.190) and Cumin Lamb (see p.194) baos, I want to share a vegan-friendly version for those looking to switch things up occasionally. These are jam-packed with texture and flavour, and are my favourite vegan buns.

---

- 2-3 tbsp cooking oil of choice, for frying
- 1 large handful of finely chopped spring onions (green onions)
- 2 tsp black sesame seeds
- The Ultimate Dumpling Sauce (see p.26), to serve

FOR THE DOUGH
- - - - - - - - - - - - - - - - - - - - - - - - - - - - - -

- 250g (scant 2 cups) plain (all-purpose) flour
- 1 tsp instant dried yeast
- 1 tsp granulated sugar
- 150ml (⅔ cup) lukewarm water

FOR THE FILLING
- - - - - - - - - - - - - - - - - - - - - - - - - - - - - -

- 1 tbsp cooking oil of choice
- 1 carrot, finely diced
- ½ courgette (zucchini), finely diced
- 5 chestnut mushrooms, finely chopped
- 4 shiitake mushrooms, finely chopped
- 1 handful of chopped spring onions (green onions)
- 150g (5½oz) block of firm tofu, drained well and crumbled
- 1 tbsp light soy sauce
- 2 tbsp hoisin sauce
- 1 tsp sesame oil
- 1 tsp minced garlic
- 1 tbsp cornflour (cornstarch)
- ½ tsp salt

**MAKING THE DOUGH** Combine the flour with the yeast and sugar in a large mixing bowl. Gradually pour in the water, mixing with a wooden spoon to make a ragged dough. Knead on a lightly floured surface for a minute until it comes together into a rough ball. Place the dough back in the bowl, cover with a damp tea (dish) towel or cling film (plastic wrap). Leave the dough to rise in a warm place until doubled in size, about 1–2 hours depending on the room temperature.

**MAKING THE FILLING** Heat the cooking oil in a large frying pan and sauté the prepared vegetables and tofu with all the seasoning ingredients, except the cornflour. Mix the cornflour with 2 tablespoons of water, then add to the pan. Stir and heat through until the liquid in the pan has thickened. Tip the filling into a bowl and leave to cool until needed.

**SHAPING THE WRAPPERS** Once the dough has risen, punch out the air and knead several times on a lightly floured surface until a smoothish ball of dough. Pierce a hole all the way through the centre of the dough with your thumb and begin stretching out the hole until it forms a large ring doughnut shape. Make a cut in the "doughnut" with a knife to open it out into a log. Roll the log out until the circumference of your forefinger at its fattest point, then divide it into 20 pieces. Cover with a damp tea towel or cling film to prevent the pieces drying out.

**FILLING AND PLEATING** Follow the instructions for the Pork & Leek Sheng Jian Baos (see p.190). Repeat until all the wrappers are filled and pleated. Cover the filled and shaped baos as you work through the dough to prevent them drying out – they may rise a little as the dough is yeasted.

**COOKING** Heat 1 tablespoon of the cooking oil in a large frying pan (with a lid) on a medium heat. Before the oil is too hot, arrange the baos slightly spaced out in the pan and cook in batches for 7 minutes, or until the bottoms are golden brown and crisp. Pour enough water into the pan, so it's 1cm (½in) deep. Cover with the lid and let the baos steam for 4–5 minutes, until the liquid is absorbed and the filling cooked through. Remove from the pan, then cook the second batch, adding another 1 tablespoon of oil. Cook a third batch of the baos in the same way, if needed.

Once all the baos are cooked, place them on a serving plate and scatter the spring onions and sesame seeds over, if using. Enjoy with the dumpling sauce by the side.

**SERVES 4**
(MAKES 25–30)

# Pork & Prawn Wontons

鲜 虾 猪 肉 馄 饨

● PREP: 1 HOUR    ● COOK: 30 MINS

Another delicious kind of dumpling, wontons have a much thinner dough than potstickers or baos, wrapped around a filling which has almost the same texture as a meatball. In Chinese cuisine, wontons are often served in a lightly seasoned broth (see p.202).

Shaping wontons is much easier than pleating dumplings or baos, so this is a great one to get started with. The filling is a classic combination of finely chopped pork and prawn (shrimp) but, as with the dumplings, you can customize the filling to suit your personal preference.

Like the dumplings, you can also freeze the wontons to enjoy another day. Follow the same method for freezing as the Chicken Potstickers on page 186.

---

- 25–30 pre-made wonton wrappers, about 200g (7oz) pack
- The Ultimate Dumpling Sauce (see p.26), to serve, optional

FOR THE FILLING

- 150g (5½oz) pork shoulder, finely chopped
- 150g (5½oz) raw shelled king prawns (shrimp), deveined and minced
- 1 egg
- ½ tsp sesame oil, plus extra to serve
- 1 tbsp light soy sauce, plus extra to serve
- 25g (1oz) spring onions (green onions), finely chopped
- ¼ tsp ground white pepper

**MAKING THE FILLING** Mix all the ingredients in a bowl, stirring continuously with a fork in one direction for 4 minutes, until combined. Stirring in one direction helps the protein strands to bind together more quickly. If you want to taste test at this point, fry a spoonful of the mixture until cooked through and adjust the seasoning, if needed.

**FILLING AND PLEATING** Take a wonton wrapper and place a teaspoon of filling into the centre. Wet the edges with your finger using a little bit of water.

**SHAPE 1** Scrunch the wrapper around the filling to form a little pouch (see opposite) and set aside.

**SHAPE 2** Fold the wrapper in half diagonally over the filling to make a triangle, squeezing out any air around the filling as you press the edges together to seal. Now wet the two corners furthest away from each other, along where the fold is made with a little more water and fold the two corners into the middle to meet (see p.201).

Repeat with the rest of the wontons and filling, choosing shape 1 or 2 as preferred.

**COOKING** Boil, steam, or deep-fry the wontons, following the instructions on page 189. Serve the wontons with soy sauce and sesame oil and/or my dumpling sauce.

# Chilli Oil Wontons

●
PREP:
5 MINS

●
COOK:
10 MINS

If you've got a batch of leftover fresh or frozen homemade wontons (see p.198) to hand now is the time to put them to good use in this simple, yet classic, Sichuan-style dish.

Here, the plump, juicy pork and prawn (shrimp)-filled wontons come tossed in a spicy, tangy sauce. Feel free to adjust the sauce to your preferred level of spice by adding more or less of the signature deep-red Sichuan chilli oil.

- 16 Pork & Prawn Wontons (see p.198) or shop-bought alternative
- 1 handful of chopped spring onions (green onions)

FOR THE SAUCE

- 2 tbsp Sichuan Chilli Oil (see p.24), or to taste
- 2 tbsp light soy sauce
- 2 tbsp Chinese black vinegar
- 1 tbsp sesame oil

PAIRING SUGGESTIONS

- Egg Drop Soup (see p.38)
- Shanghai Spring Onion Oil Noodles (see p.42)

Bring a large pan of water to the boil and add the wontons. (You may have to cook them in two batches, depending on how big the pan is.) Bring the water back to a gentle boil and cook for 5 minutes, until the wontons float to the surface.

Remove the wontons with a slotted spoon, drain and place the first batch in a serving dish while you cook the second batch.

In a separate bowl, mix all the ingredients for the sauce together.

Pour the sauce over the cooked wontons and turn gently until they are coated in the sauce.

Scatter over the spring onions and serve with egg drop soup and Shanghai spring onion oil noodles for a more substantial meal.

BONUS

This wonton shape is popular as it resembles old Chinese ingots, known as yuanbao (元宝).

# Wonton Noodle Soup

**PREP:**
5 MINS*

**COOK:**
10 MINS

*plus soaking mushrooms

Another great way to enjoy wontons is to serve them in a noodle soup. Wonton noodle soups are popular across Southeast Asia, but it is thought that they originated in the Canton region of China. This noodle soup is one I enjoyed growing up. For me, slurping on slippery wontons alongside thin, chewy noodles is the ultimate internal hug, and perfect for when it's cold outside.

Assuming you've already done the hard work of making the Pork & Prawn Wontons from scratch (see p.198), you can whip this soup up in as little as 15 minutes. Alternatively, substitute the homemade wontons for shop-bought ones.

---

- 4-5 dried or fresh shiitake mushrooms, thinly sliced
- 200g (7oz) dried thin egg noodles or 400g (14oz) fresh wonton noodles
- 10-15 fresh or frozen Pork & Prawn Wontons (see p.198) or shop-bought frozen alternative
- 1 litre (4¼ cups) chicken or vegetable stock
- 1 pak choi (bok choy), leaves separated
- 2 tbsp light soy sauce
- 1 tsp sesame oil
- salt, to taste
- pinch of MSG, optional
- 1 handful of chopped spring onions (green onions)

If using dried shiitake mushrooms, put them in a heatproof bowl and pour over enough just-boiled water from a kettle to cover. Leave to soak for 10 minutes, until rehydrated, then drain well and thinly slice.

Meanwhile, cook the noodles in a pan of boiling water according to the packet instructions. Drain and rinse briefly under cold running water, then divide between two serving bowls. You may want to boil the wontons with the noodles if they're fresh. If your wontons are frozen, cook them for 1–2 minutes before you add the noodles. Alternatively, cook the wontons in a separate large pan of boiling water, then drain and refresh under cold running water.

In a separate pan, bring the stock to a gentle boil. Add the fresh or dried shiitake mushrooms and pak choi leaves and blanch for 2 minutes. Using a slotted spoon, remove the pak choi and mushrooms and place in the serving bowls on top of the noodles and wontons.

Season the stock with soy sauce, sesame oil, salt and MSG, if using.

Ladle the soup broth into the serving bowls and sprinkle with the spring onions before serving.

# Mango Sticky Rice

PREP:
15 MINS*

COOK:
45 MINS

*plus soaking the rice

This probably needs little in the way of introduction as it is one of the most popular and well-known Asian desserts. What's more, the simple Thai pudding of juicy mango and fragrant coconut rice is surprisingly easy to make at home, which I discovered during lockdown in the first wave of the 2020 pandemic.

I had recently returned from a trip to Thailand and was missing the delicious street food. Having taken for granted how easy it was to pick up a portion of delicious mango sticky rice from a street vendor, I set myself the challenge of learning how to make it. It was a fabulous day when I tucked into my first bowlful of the dessert after dreaming about it for so long.

- 250g (1¼ cups) Thai sticky rice (glutinous rice)
- 400g (14oz) can full-fat coconut milk
- 80-125g (6½-10 tbsp) granulated sugar, to taste
- 1 tbsp cornflour (cornstarch)
- 1-2 ripe mangoes, peeled, stone removed and chopped into small chunks or slices
- ½ tsp toasted sesame seeds
- a few mint leaves, to decorate, optional

Wash the rice thoroughly under cold running water until the water runs clear. Tip the rice into a large bowl and pour in enough water to cover generously. Leave to soak for at least 6 hours, ideally overnight.

Meanwhile, line a steamer basket with baking (parchment) paper large enough to hold and cover the rice. Drain the rice and place in the lined steamer, then fold over the baking paper to enclose it in a sort of parcel. Cover with the lid and steam for 30–40 minutes, until the rice is cooked and fluffy. (If you don't have a steamer, use a metal colander in a pan half-filled with water.)

While the rice is steaming, gently heat the coconut milk with the sugar (starting with the smallest amount and adding more, to taste) in a small pan, stirring occasionally, until the sugar dissolves.

Once the rice is cooked and the texture is soft, unwrap the baking paper parcel and transfer the rice to a bowl. Pour three-quarters of the sweetened coconut milk over the rice and mix through with a fork. The rice will absorb a lot of the liquid in time, so don't worry if it looks a bit runny at first.

Add the cornflour to the remaining sweetened coconut milk and gently heat, stirring continuously until thickened to a syrup consistency. This is the coconut milk syrup.

To serve, spoon the coconut sticky rice into a serving bowl and top with the chopped or sliced mango. Drizzle over the coconut milk syrup and sprinkle with sesame seeds and mint, if using.

# Mango Pomelo Sago

PREP:
15 MINS

COOK:
30 MINS

This twist on the popular Hong Kong dessert combines small tapioca pearls with fresh mango and pomelo in a sweet coconut-mango milk. The traditional recipe is made with a combination of evaporated milk and coconut milk, but this vegan version uses just the latter.

The citrus flavour of the pomelo really helps to balance the sweetness, making this dessert super refreshing and perfect for summer. Tastewise, pomelo is similar to grapefruit, but a little less sour and tangy. If you can't find it, feel free to substitute with grapefruit instead. Alternatively, I've made this without the citrus element before, and it still tastes fantastic.

- 150g (5½oz) small white tapioca pearls
- 400ml (1¾ cups) full-fat coconut milk (or replace half with evaporated milk)
- 3 tbsp granulated sugar
- ¼ tsp salt
- ½ tsp vanilla extract
- 2 ripe mangoes
- 100g (3½oz) pomelo or grapefruit, segmented
- 6 small sprigs of fresh mint, to decorate

Bring 1 litre (4⅓ cups) of water to the boil in a saucepan and add the tapioca. Turn the heat down to low, stir to mix with a spatula and simmer for 20 minutes, or until most of the tapioca pearls are no longer white and become translucent. Stir occasionally to prevent the tapioca sticking or burning on the bottom of the pan.

While the tapioca is cooking, gently heat the coconut milk in a separate pan with the sugar and salt, stirring occasionally until dissolved. Add the vanilla, stir to combine and set aside to cool.

Once the tapioca is cooked, drain over a sieve and stir with a spoon to remove any excess liquid. This may take a few minutes as the texture is a little gloopy. Add the cooked tapioca to the sweetened coconut milk and mix thoroughly. Transfer to a lidded container and place in the fridge to cool while you prepare the mango.

Peel each mango with a vegetable peeler and carefully cut the fruit away around the central stone in large chunks. Purée half of the chopped mango in a blender until smooth. Combine the purée with the pomelo or grapefruit segments and set aside in a bowl. Cut the rest of the mango into small cubes and set aside for later.

To serve, take a glass and spoon in a layer of the mango pomelo purée, followed by coconut tapioca. Place some chopped mango on top and decorate with a mint sprig. There is enough for 6 servings, but any leftovers can be kept in the fridge in an airtight container for 2–3 days.

# Matcha Burnt Basque Cheesecake

● ●
PREP:   COOK:
20 MINS*  45 MINS

*plus chilling, optional

If you asked a room full of people to name their favourite dessert, chances are a fair number would say a good cheesecake. I don't blame them - what's not to love about the combination of cream, cheese and sugar? This recipe is a take on the famous Spanish burnt Basque cheesecake, which has a more rustic appearance than the New York version.

The first time I made a burnt Basque cheesecake, it was for a first date. We'd agreed to go on a picnic for the occasion and he casually mentioned, as he listed all the things he was going to bring, that he was coeliac. Coincidentally, I'd been meaning to try this cheesecake recipe for ages, and, of course, I did, and it was a big hit.

That summer, I spent many hours perfecting the recipe, because my first few attempts weren't quite as I'd hoped, but I got there in the end. So, here I present to you one of my top desserts to make at home, and a matcha version, just because I love all things matcha. The cheesecake is flourless, meaning it's perfect for coeliacs and those on a gluten-free diet.

- 400g (scant 2 cups) cream cheese
- 145g (¾ cup) caster (superfine) sugar
- 2 large eggs
- 300ml (1¼ cups) double (heavy) cream
- ½ tsp vanilla extract
- 3 tbsp gluten-free cornflour (cornstarch)
- 1 tbsp good-quality matcha tea powder
- pinch of salt

Preheat the oven to 220°C/200°C fan/425°F/Gas 7. Line the base and sides of a deep loose-bottomed 18cm (6in) cake tin with 2 large sheets of baking (parchment) paper, one of the sheets turned at 45 degrees, so the corners point in different directions. Next, press the paper into the tin and fold over any paper protruding above the rim of the cake tin – this will help you lift the cheesecake out after baking. Don't worry about any creases as they add to the character of the cheesecake.

In a stand mixer or using a hand whisk, manual or electric, combine the cream cheese and sugar in a large mixing bowl until smooth. Add the eggs, one at a time, and mix together thoroughly.

Next, add the cream and vanilla to the cream-cheese mixture and whisk until everything is well combined, scraping down the sides a few times with a spatula to help.

Mix the cornflour, matcha powder and salt together in a bowl, then gradually sift the mixture into the cream mixture and told it in making sure there are no lumps and it's well incorporated.

Matcha powder can be lumpy, so sifting it with the cornflour helps to achieve an ultra-smooth consistency.

Pour the matcha mixture into the prepared cake tin, tap the tin on the work surface to make sure there are no air bubbles and level the top.

Bake the cheesecake for 30–45 minutes, depending on your oven. I always start with 30 minutes to check how much colour there is on top – you want it to look fairly dark and puffed up like a soufflé. Insert a skewer into the centre to check the cheesecake is ready; the middle should be a little runny when fully cooked but not too wet. If you gently shake the tin from side-to-side, the cheesecake should have a slight wobble, but will firm up once cool and continue to set in the refrigerator. Continue to bake the cheesecake for a further 10–15 minutes if it isn't ready, keeping an eye on it as you go.

Once cooked, remove the cheesecake from the oven and let it cool in the tin to room temperature. It will collapse slightly in the middle as it cools.

You can eat the cheesecake at this stage when still slightly gooey in the middle, or chill in the fridge for a couple of hours until ready to eat.

BONUS

P.S. You can totally omit the matcha powder in this recipe and still produce an incredibly delicious burnt Basque cheesecake.

# Fried Milk

● ●
**PREP:** **COOK:**
**30 MINS*** **20 MINS**

*plus chilling

I grew up on milk desserts as a child. My parents believed in the benefits of consuming dairy, and how it contributed to me growing taller and giving me healthy bones. This milky dessert originates from the Guangdong Province, a coastal region in the southeast of China, though I learnt through travelling that there are similar dishes elsewhere in the world, including some Hispanic countries.

Unlike the Hispanic version, the Chinese one doesn't contain cinnamon, which is normally reserved for savoury dishes, and it's traditionally made without the crumb coating. These days, however, the breadcrumbed version is more popular as it gives the fried milk a crispy textured coating and golden appearance. I think it's more delicious, too.

---

- 200ml (scant 1 cup) whole milk
- 2 tbsp cornflour (cornstarch)
- 2 tbsp caster (superfine) sugar
- 100ml (6½ tbsp) cooking oil of choice
- 2 tbsp plain (all-purpose) flour
- 1 egg
- 50g (1 cup) panko breadcrumbs
- 1 tsp icing (confectioners') sugar, for dusting, optional

Pour the milk into a small pan and sift in the cornflour and sugar. With a balloon whisk, whisk everything together until combined and bring the milk to a gentle simmer on a low heat. Stir continuously until the mixture starts to thicken, then cook for another 3–4 minutes, until a thick paste. Remove from the heat.

Grease a 20 x 12cm (8 x 5in) rectangular baking dish or glass/plastic container with a little of the cooking oil and spoon in the milk mixture. Shake the dish or container from side-to-side a few times until the milk mixture is level, then smooth the top with a palette knife. Ideally the mixture should be about 1 cm (½in) deep. Cover and chill for 20 minutes, or until the milk mixture has set solid. Turn out the solidified milk block onto a chopping board and cut into bite-sized pieces.

Put the flour in a shallow dish and whisk the egg in a bowl. Put the breadcrumbs in a separate shallow dish. To breadcrumb the milk pieces, dust them first in the flour until lightly coated, then dip into the whisked egg. Lastly, press them into the breadcrumbs until coated. Set aside. Repeat until all the milk pieces are covered.

Heat the cooking oil in a large frying pan on a medium–high heat until hot. In batches, add the crumbed milk pieces and shallow fry for 3–5 minutes, until golden brown and crispy, turning over halfway. (You can also do this in a deep-fat fryer, if you have one.) Drain briefly on kitchen paper to remove any excess oil, while you cook the rest of the pieces. The fried milk can be enjoyed as is or with a dusting of icing sugar. Eat while still hot!

# Mochi

## PREP: 15 MINS*    COOK: 10 MINS

*plus cooling and chilling

Many of you will be familiar with the filled rice flour balls, known as mochi, thanks to the viral videos of Japanese men pounding mochi dough with a wooden hammer. Though you and I may not be armed with the same tools, I can assure you that it's entirely possible to make delicious mochi at home. And best of all, no steamer basket is necessary, as I'm going to show you how to make them in the microwave.

---

### FOR THE MOCHI DOUGH

- 165g (heaped 1¼ cups) glutinous rice flour
- 65g (⅓ cup) caster (superfine) sugar

### FOR THE FILLING

- 80g (scant ⅔ cup) roasted unsalted peanuts, crushed to a coarse crumb
- 1 tbsp pure coconut oil
- 1 tbsp peanut butter, smooth or crunchy
- 1 tbsp desiccated (shredded) coconut, plus extra for coating
- 1 tbsp caster (superfine) sugar

Start to make the mochi dough, mix the rice flour and sugar with 340ml (scant 1½ cups) water in a microwaveable mixing bowl until smooth.

Cover the mixing bowl with cling film (plastic wrap) and microwave at the highest setting for about 5–6 minutes, stirring halfway with a spatula, until it becomes a firm, sticky dough. It is fully cooked when the dough turns slightly translucent and smooth. You can taste test a little to see if it is still grainy. If so, microwave for a further 2-3 minutes. (This is optional: when the dough is ready, pound it with the end of a rolling pin to make the texture of the mochi extra chewy.) Set aside and leave to cool in the bowl while you make the filling.

Mix all the ingredients for the filling together until the mixture resembles rough wet sand. Set aside.

Generously scatter extra desiccated coconut into a shallow dish to cover the mochi and place a bowl of warm water nearby.

To shape the mochi, scoop out a large tablespoon of the cooled dough and drop it into the coconut. Dip your fingers into the warm water and press the dough to flatten it slightly to make space for the filling. Spoon 1 tablespoon of the peanut mixture into the middle, then carefully pinch the edges of the dough around the filling to make a ball. Dip your fingers in more water if the dough becomes too sticky.

Roll the mochi in more coconut until coated and repeat to make 10 balls in total. Enjoy straightaway or store in an airtight container for 3–4 days.

## Set Menu

→ PICKLED CUCUMBER (27)

→ CHINESE SPRING ONION PANCAKES (172)

→ TERIYAKI CHICKEN SKEWERS (182)

# Index

# Acknowledgments

To myself, for just getting on with it, and life, and never giving up.

To my family, for the work ethic and discipline they instilled in me from a young age, and for always pushing me to aim higher.

To all my closest friends, for supporting me in your individual ways when I was getting started, and for being my biggest supporters throughout this journey. Cheers for always being up for being fed by me and loving my cooking.

To my therapist, Leann, for guiding me and my life so that I can focus my mental energy on the right places.

To my agent, Kemi, for finding me and believing in me more than I ever did myself, and for your tireless efforts in getting my work in front of the right people.

To my publisher Katie and the DK team, Cara, Tania and Lucy, for running with my idea and making this book a tangible reality. To designers Emma and Nikki, and to my editor, Nicola, for turning my candid thoughts into eloquent paragraphs and stories.

To my photography dream team, Lizzie, Elliya, Flossy and Sophie, this book would be nowhere near as beautiful without your magic. I'm incredibly grateful for the intricate detail that went into each dish and photograph.

To my online community from every corner of the world. Thank you for everything, from trying my recipes and sharing your words of appreciation. I read every single message and this book would not have been possible without all of you.

To all the guys I dated throughout the years, as every time the topic of passions came up, it reiterated to myself how much I loved this side gig of mine, which is now my entire life and livelihood.

And to my cats, Peanut and Hazel, who will probably take one sniff at the book and never bat an eyelid at it ever again - thanks for all the moral support in your feline ways.

**Editor** Nicola Graimes
**Designer** Emma Wells, Studio Nic&Lou
**Photographer** Lizzie Mayson
**Food Stylist** Flossy McAslan
**Prop Stylist** Charlie Phillips
**Proofreader** Katie Hardwicke
**Indexer** Angie Hipkin

**DK LONDON**
**Project Editor** Lucy Sienkowska
**Senior Designer** Tania Gomes
**Senior Production Editor** Tony Phipps
**Production Controller** Rebecca Parton
**Jacket Coordinator** Jasmin Lennie
**Editorial Director** Cara Armstrong
**Publishing Director** Katie Cowan
**Art Director** Maxine Pedliham

First published in Great Britain in 2023 by
Dorling Kindersley Limited
DK, One Embassy Gardens, 8 Viaduct Gardens,
London, SW11 7BW

The authorised representative in the EEA is
Dorling Kindersley Verlag GmbH. Arnulfstr. 124,
80636 Munich, Germany

Illustrations contain elements of Shutterstock.com:
Julia Kovryzhenko; Mari Muzz; RioRita.

A CIP catalogue record for this book
is available from the British Library.
ISBN: 978-0-2416-2028-1

Printed and bound in Slovakia

**For the curious**
**www.dk.com**

MIX
Paper | Supporting
responsible forestry
FSC™ C018179

This book was made with Forest
Stewardship Council™ certified
paper – one small step in DK's
commitment to a sustainable future.
**For more information go to**
www.dk.com/our-green-pledge